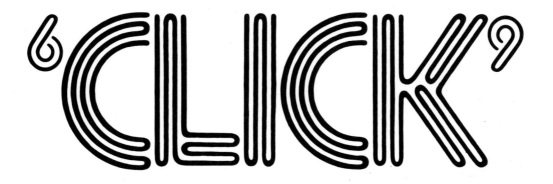

'CLICK'

Russell Miller

ARCO PUBLISHING COMPANY, INC.
New York

Credits

David Bailey	54
Harry Bakkers	101
Cecil Beaton	56, 57, 120
Mike Berkofsky	84
Lester Bookbinder	111
Margaret Bourke-White (Time Life/Colorific)	64 bottom, 106-7
Michael Boys	85
Bill Brandt	70, 71, 86, 87, 114, 115
Camera Press	119
Robert Capa (Magnum)	65 top, 66, 67 top
H. Cartier-Bresson (Magnum)	65 bottom, 69
Bruce Coleman (Joseph Van Wormer)	102
Colorific	(Don Hunstein) opposite title page, Carl Purcell 12 bottom left, 32, 37 bottom left
Tony Copeland	112-3
Gerry Cranham	13 bottom left, 14, 15
H. E. Edgerton	8, 10, 11
Mary Evans Picture Library	28 top, 29 top, 75
John Garrett	83
John Goldblatt	96
C. Gouweleeuw	18
H. Grooteclaes	19
Steve Herr	117, end papers
Eric Howard	108-9
Karsh (Camera Press)	52
Kodak Museum	23 top and centre left, 24, 30 top right, 31, 33, 36 bottom
Patrick Lichfield	55, 82 (courtesy Bayer Pharmaceuticals)
Angus McBean	53 bottom, 110
Don McCullin (Sunday Times)	67 bottom
Mansell Collection	46, 47, 76 top left and bottom left
Duane Michals	53 top
Toby Molenaar	97
Lennart Nilsson (Time Life/Colorific)	20, 21
Roger Phillips	100
Picturepoint	12 bottom right
Punch	26
Radio Times Hulton Picture Library	23 bottom left and bottom right, 29 bottom, 30 top left, 36 top right, 51 top, 59, 61, 90, 92 bottom, 76
Malcolm Robertson	12 top, 116
Ronan Picture Library	28 bottom, 30 centre left, 34, 35, 37 top and bottom right
Royal Photographic Society	6, 25 bottom, 30 centre right, 38, 39 top, 40 top left and bottom, 42-3, 45, 48, 49, 50, 51 bottom left, 63, 68, 77, 78, 79, 80, 89, 91, 92 top, 93, 94, 95, 103
Science Museum, London	Opposite contents, top 3, 24
Eugene Smith (Time Life/Colorific)	64 top
Snark	40 top right, 41
Snowdon	72, 73
Howard Sochurek (John Hillelson Agency,	16-17
Victoria and Albert Museum	61 bottom, 62, 76 right
H. Roger Viollet	36 top left, 118
James Wedge	13 bottom right
Edward Weston (Courtesy Cole Weston)	81, 98, 99
Adam Woolfitt	104-5

Front cover Photograph: Roger Phillips, Radio Times Hulton Picture Library

A—1796

Published by Arco Publishing Company, Inc.
219 Park Avenue South, New York, N.Y. 10003

Copyright © 1974 by Marshall Cavendish Publications Limited

All rights reserved

Library of Congress Catalog Card Number 74-76267

ISBN 0-668-03485-x

Printed in Great Britain

About this book

Few inventions have enriched the human experience
more than photography. This is undoubtedly so.
But what of its history and scope ? When was it
first invented and by whom ? How can it be used as an
aid to technological advancement and in medical
diagnosis ? Is it in fact an art form ?

These are just a few of the many intriguing questions
to which you'll find lavishly illustrated answers
in CLICK.

Let this compelling collection of photographs tell an
exciting visual story in black and white, and colour.
Seven highly entertaining, information-packed
chapters present flashbacks to the camera's early
years, including examples of nude photography
and portraiture both yesterday and today. Meet the
'concerned' photographers, those committed men and women
who capture in graphic detail the plight of the poor
and forgotten, the state of people at war. Discover,
too, how certain dramatic effects are achieved, and
marvel at the work of some of the world's top
names in photography — Bill Brandt, Lord Snowdon,
Cecil Beaton, Karsh, Cartier-Bresson and Robert Capa
among them.

Contents

VIEWS, ARCHITECTURE, &c.

STATUARY, STILL LIFE &c.

SINGLE PORTRAITS & GROUPS

MR BEARD,
(SOLE PATENTEE)
OF THE
DAGUERREOTYPE
OR
Photographic Portraiture.

34, PARLIAMENT S! WESTMINSTER,
85, KING WILLIAM S! CITY,
&
ROYAL POLYTECHNIC INSTITUTION
309, REGENT ST. LONDON.

Here is an agent in Photography by which the much prized family Portrait the old cherished Picture may be multiplied at a trivial cost & with such exactness & truth as to establish an identity of character the minutest detail may be perfectly represented.

As well for momentary expression of countenance as for drapery in elaborate patterns, for chased Armour, carved furniture, articles of Vertu whether of Marble or Silver, indeed for every description of still life the Photographic principle has been successfully employed.

The art of Photography is indeed as great a step in the fine arts as the steam engine was in the mechanical arts, it has called to its aid the highest resources of chemistry and Physics.

Edinburgh. Rev.

"Could we now see in Photogenic light & shade, Demosthenes launching his thunders against Macedon, or Paul preaching in Athens, with what rapture should we gaze upon impersonations so exciting! The heroes & sages of ancient times, would thus have been embalmed with more than Egyptian skill."
EDINBURGH. REV.

"The progress made in bringing, we might say to perfection, this surprising discovery must stagger the most incredulous. The fleshy hue & tints, the play of emotion, the glow of breathing life are all embodied."
Times.

"It was color that was wanting to crown the improvements. Then was obtained what had been so often sought for a speaking likeness." No matter how delicate the tint, how bright the glow, the color was communicated.

Techniques

Few inventions have broadened the scope of human knowledge more than that of photography. In its simplest form it has shown us the wonders of the world and faithfully recorded the day-by-day passage of modern history.

But its achievements are far greater than just that. With the camera we have been able to explore the heavens beyond the scope of the most powerful telescope. We have been able to observe life in the deepest oceans. We are able to see the development, in the womb, of a human baby. We have discovered how horses gallop and bats fly. We have been able to decipher the Dead Sea Scrolls and manufacture electronic circuits with 500,000 components to the square inch — all because of the invention of photography.

So much has been achieved through photography that it is hard to believe that the techniques which have made all this possible are still in their infancy. Before the end of this century, the two-dimensional photograph may be obsolete. Already it is possible, with the help of laser beams, to produce perfect three-dimensional images.

This process, called holography, makes a conventional black and white photograph as out-dated as a silent movie. Imagine being able to project your photographs — or holographs, rather — not on to a flat screen but into a box in which the picture appears, absolutely life-like, in three dimensions. The concept might seem almost like science-fiction, but then, at one time, a simple photograph was the object of public awe.

When the pioneers of photography produced their first efforts in the 1820s, they could not have foreseen the effects their invention would have on the world. Among scientists, the astronomers were first to realize the potential of the important discovery. Unlike the human eye, film can store light — so a camera attached to a telescope was able to 'see' further into the universe than ever before. With very long exposures — two, three and four hours — astronomers were able to take good pictures of stars they had not even known existed. It was through photography we learned that our own

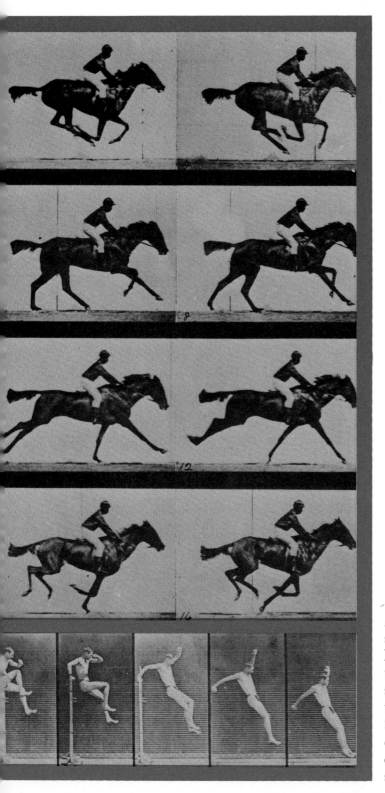

galaxy is not the centre of the universe, as had previously been thought, but just one of countless others.

Not all the discoveries made as a result of photographs were so far-reaching, but many, in their own way, were just as important. In the 1870s artists throughout the world suffered the humiliation of learning from a photograph that they had been painting horses incorrectly. An Englishman named Eadweard Muybridge, using twelve cameras tripped in sequence, obtained a series of pictures of a horse at full gallop which showed quite clearly that at times the horse had all four hooves off the ground. Until then, galloping horses had always been painted inaccurately with all four legs extended. These pictures are said to have won a 25,000 dollar bet for a rich American industrialist.

The Split-Second Strobe

The ability of the camera to 'stop' even the fastest moving action has played a significant role in learning over the last 150 years. In the early days of photography, the speed of the shutter was the limiting factor to the length of the exposure. The big breakthrough came in the 1930s, with the invention of the electronic 'strobe' light, which made exposures of one-millionth of a second possible.

Like many of the best inventions, the idea is basically simple. A strobe light can flash much faster than the fastest mechanical shutter. Under ordinary lighting conditions, with a lens stopped down to its smallest aperture and the shutter set at its fastest speed, very little light enters the camera.

Left **A silhouette-like series of photographs shows exactly how a horse gallops. In 1877, Eadweard Muybridge brought several cameras to a track, placed strings attached to electric switches across the horse's path and allowed them to be broken as the animal raced by. Shutters were released by electromagnetic control at a speed, so Muybridge exaggerated, of one two-thousandth of a second. Similar series illustrate human locomotion.**

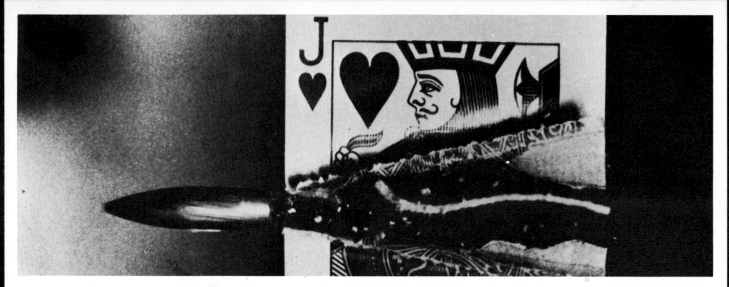

A bullet cuts the Knave of Hearts in Harold Edgerton's famous high speed action shot.

But with a strobe light coupled to the shutter, the length of its brilliant flash gives an effective exposure.

With the help of strobe lights, new realms were opened up to photographers. They were able to 'stop' the wings of humming birds, previously only seen as a blur. They were able to find beauty in the most everyday things — the patterns formed by a drop of milk splashing into a saucer or water running from a tap.

One of the pioneers in this field was the man largely responsible for the invention of the strobe, Harold Edgerton. In a historic series of pictures using multiple strobe lights which gave him hundreds of exposures every second, he was able to record the movements of golfers and tennis players. It was his photographs which proved that a golfer's 'follow through' stroke is irrelevant — the ball leaves the club the instant it is struck. Professor Edgerton, an American, also took many astonishing photographs of bullets in flight. These pictures showed, for the first time, that a bullet 'splashes' on impact — when it hits a solid object it liquefies for an instant and then reforms.

Unlimited Versatility

As well as being able to stop the fastest movement, the camera also has the ability to speed up the slowest movement. By exposing a picture every hour, every day or even every week, the camera is able to record the way a bud blossoms into flower or the various stages in the life-cycle of a tiny insect. Scientists can observe the formation of rust or the development of mildew; astronomers can detect, by time lapse photographs recording the movements of a star over a number of years, how many satellites are orbiting around it.

Few of the tools available to contemporary society are as versatile as the camera. As well as being able to see far beyond the boundaries of the human eye, it can also look at life more closely. Photographs produced with the aid of a scanning electron microscope can produce an image up to 140,000 times life-size. Thus the ordinary becomes extraordinary — a fine thread almost invisible to the naked eye becomes a thick rope, an apparently smooth surface appears pitted and cratered like the surface of the moon, the jaws of an ant assume nightmare proportions and detail. In the study of fibres, bacteria and insect life, such photographs have been invaluable.

At the other end of the scale from photographing at such close quarters is the technique of aerial photography. Early photographers mounted their equipment in balloons and sent it up simply to get a bird's eye view of their surroundings — today aerial photography has a more serious purpose than mere curiosity.

With the help of photographs taken from the air, ecologists can study the effects of pollution both of air and water, geologists can pinpoint the likely sources of water, oil and minerals, naturalists can study the behaviour of animals and count their population, town planners can foresee more clearly the pattern of future development . . . and countries can spy on one another.

Aerial photographs taken by a U2 spy-plane revealed the presence of Russian missiles in Cuba in 1962 and precipitated the crisis that brought the world to the brink of war. From a height of nearly 12 miles the cameras fitted in U2 planes produced reconnaissance pictures so detailed that the sleepers on railway lines were clearly visible.

Photographing the Invisible

Perhaps the greatest photographic aid to man resulted from the realization that the camera was able to see and record rays of light and sound waves invisible to the human eye and to see *through* materials which the naked eye registers as solid.

In the mid-1890s a German professor called Wilhelm Röntgen was experimenting with a device called a Crookes tube, which produced a glow when electricity was passed between two electrodes in the tube. It also produced a strange radiation which he could not identify — he called them X-rays, 'X' for unknown.

One day, during the course of his investigation, Professor Röntgen put his hand between the tube and a fluorescent screen and immediately saw a shadowy image of his bones. He then discovered that the X-rays had fogged photographic plates stored in a wooden drawer. That same day, Professor Röntgen produced the world's first X-ray photograph. This discovery was hailed as the wonder of the age, as well as being the cause of some consternation when it was learned that X-rays could pass through clothes. Victorian ladies saw the invention as a severe threat to their modesty.

Before the inherent dangers of X-rays were appreciated — prolonged exposure can destroy living cells in the body and can cause cancer — they were immediately put to use by the medical world, as well as the entertainment business. Travelling fairs set up X-ray booths to demonstrate the 'greatest scientific discovery of the age' — 'by the aid of a new light you are enabled to see through a sheet of metal.'

Today X-ray photography is put to more constructive use. In the study of art it has been invaluable in exposing forgeries, revealing unknown paintings under other works and for showing how an artist's concept of his work developed.

Very hard gamma rays — a much later development of X-rays — showed how the famous mask of Tutankhamen was constructed. They are also used by industry to detect flaws in metal and to test the stress in building construction.

In science, X-rays are located beyond the violet end of the visible colour spectrum. Beyond the other end are different invisible rays which are also widely employed in photography, of which the best known are infra-red.

Infra-red rays, those sensed as heat, were known long before the discovery of X-rays but were not used in photography until the 1930s when it was found that certain dyes added to the emulsion of film would record infra-red light.

Photographs taken by infra-red light have been a revelation in many fields. In medicine, for example, they can reveal the condition of veins just under the skin. Historians use infra-red photographs to read writing on ancient documents which has faded over the years and become invisible to the naked eye. The Dead Sea Scrolls, 2,000 years old and blackened by age to illegibility, were deciphered with the help of infra-red photography.

Infra-red flashbulbs enable pictures to be taken in the dark and are frequently used by police forces throughout the world. Many an intruder has been identified by tripping a pre-set infra-red flashlight camera and being photographed red-handed without being aware of it. Infra-red light is, of course, invisible.

Pictures taken by infra-red film show colours quite differently from those registered by the human brain — the blue sky turns a brilliant green and green leaves become flaming red. Many photographers have used the technique purely as a form of artistic expression, but it has a scientific and technical value, too.

Healthy, living foliage shows up as red in an infra-red photograph; if it is dying it appears brown, so ecologists can use aerial infra-red photographs to check the extent of disease in vegetation. In the same way they can evaluate the condition of soil or the purity of water.

Infra-red photography has made camouflage more difficult for modern armies. A battalion camouflaged in undergrowth with felled trees and foliage, was once practically invisible from the air. Today an infra-red picture will clearly indicate its position.

Possibly the most revealing and fascinating photographs ever taken by the use of modern technology are those which reveal the inner workings of the human body. A Swedish photographer named Lennart Nilsson has done more than anyone else to show us what goes on inside the body.

With specially developed equipment, he has photographed the tissues inside the fallopian tubes, where sperm and egg join to create life. In 1965, using a surgical viewing scope, he was able to photograph, for the first time, a 15-week embryo actually in its mother's womb. The mysteries of life will never seem quite the same again.

At every stage in the development of photography it must have seemed to many awe-struck onlookers that the ultimate achievement had been reached, yet each step has outshone the one before. Now a photographic process is used in industry to make tiny integrated electronic circuits for transistor radios and televisions. The camera has become an indispensable tool of technology, it has penetrated deep into the human body and far into the heavens. Where else can it go? What else can it do? These are questions no one can answer.

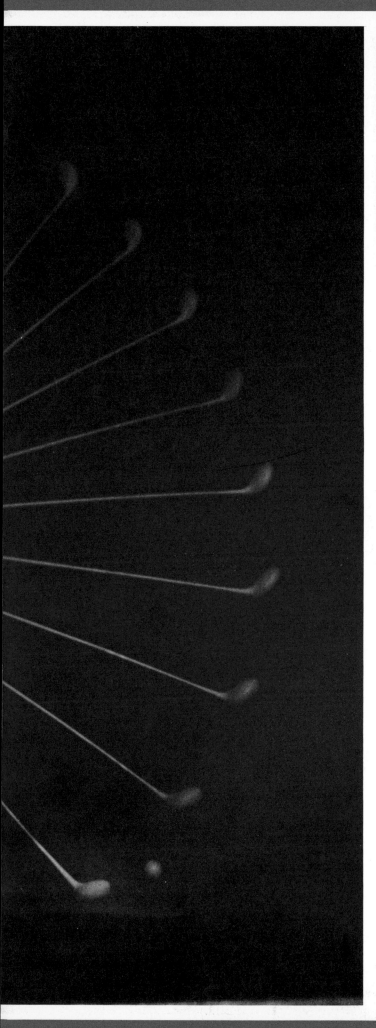

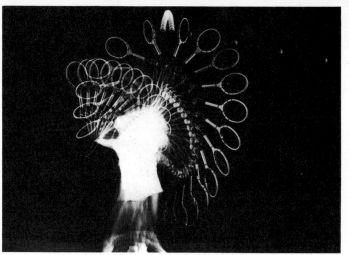

Suddenly, with photography, we enter a world not normally seen. Harold Edgerton used multiple flash to study motion as involved in sport. *Left* The astounding swing of golfer Dennis Shute. *Above* The consecutive movements forming a single, powerful tennis serve. *Overleaf top* An array of visually exciting pictures incorporating various techniques. Photographer Malcolm Robertson chose to produce the effect of multiple exposure by shooting dramatic reflections of a tiger's head in several pieces of glass. Notice how the tiger's tongue forms a rhythmic wave at each break of mirror. A wide-angle lens is basically one of shorter than normal focal length, and the resulting photographs with their distortion of natural perspective and shapes are always startlingly different. Extreme wide-angle lenses form images that closely resemble the vision of a fish.

Overleaf bottom An example of the effect of a fisheye lens is shown in the view from the schooner Seaspray, taken by Carl Purcell. Turn, too, and see how with use of macro-photography, magnification turns the transverse section of a coal fossil into a pleasing piece of abstract art. With use of three exposures, Gerry Cranham cleverly captures a few brief seconds of speeding London traffic. Creating a beauty image for the British Magazine *19*, James Wedge shows himself both photographer and artist. The girl's head and dew-laden flower were shot separately in black and white but put together to form a montage during printing. Great care was taken to ensure that lighting for both was similar.

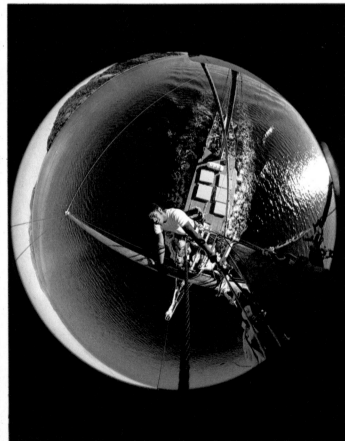

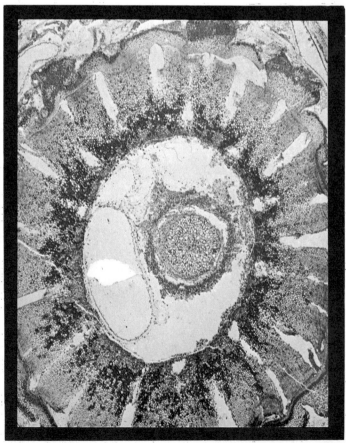

Gerry Cranham has been described as Britain's
most versatile and creative photographer
and has a world-wide reputation, too.
Above Studio shot of a cyclist taken with
two long exposures for speed lines
and movement. *Opposite* At a recent
championship meeting, Gerry Cranham
placed his camera under the trampoline and,
using a fisheye lens and remote control,
caught the descending crab-like silhouette of
a competitor, hands like pincers, at the
moment of contact with the mattress
before the form came bouncing up. *Right* The
split-second start of an all-important Women's
Athletic Association race takes on the effect of
a tremendous explosion of pent-up energy with
expert use of a special zoom lens. The technique
which involves pulling the lens inwards and a
long hand-held exposure is one which Cranham
admits took him all of five years to perfect.

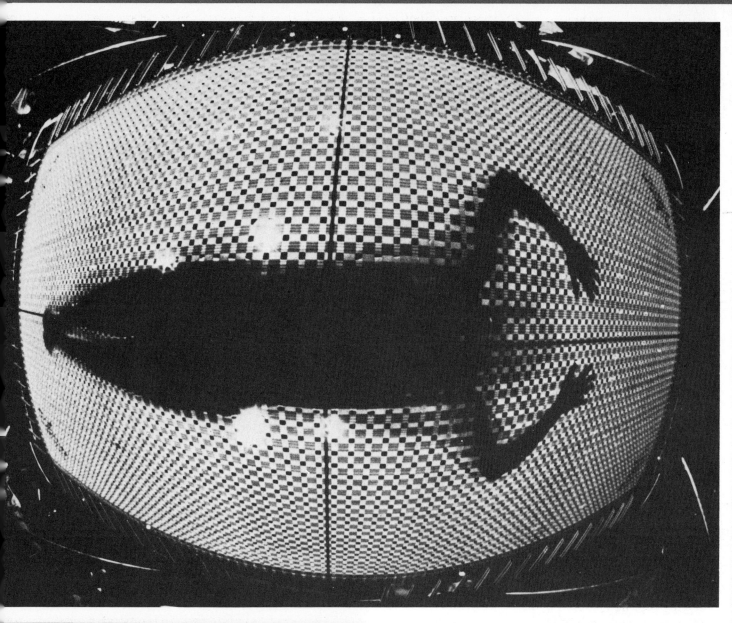

Overleaf **Using a new thermographic technique, American photographer Howard Sochurek translates heat radiation into colour, and the familiar New York skyline takes on a whole new rainbow of tones. His camera has recorded the infra-red radiation all around us — radiation emitted from atoms that form all matter: animal, vegetable and mineral. The thermographic camera responds not to light but temperature. Filters then operate to colour the mono toned image according to heat readings. Warm areas show up deep red and purple, with a gradual progression through orange, yellow, green and blue as heat decreases until the coldest parts of all are coloured black. And what of the practical uses of thermography? Its potential functions include checking of electronic equipment and reading of temperature for medical purposes. With photography, heat becomes visible.**

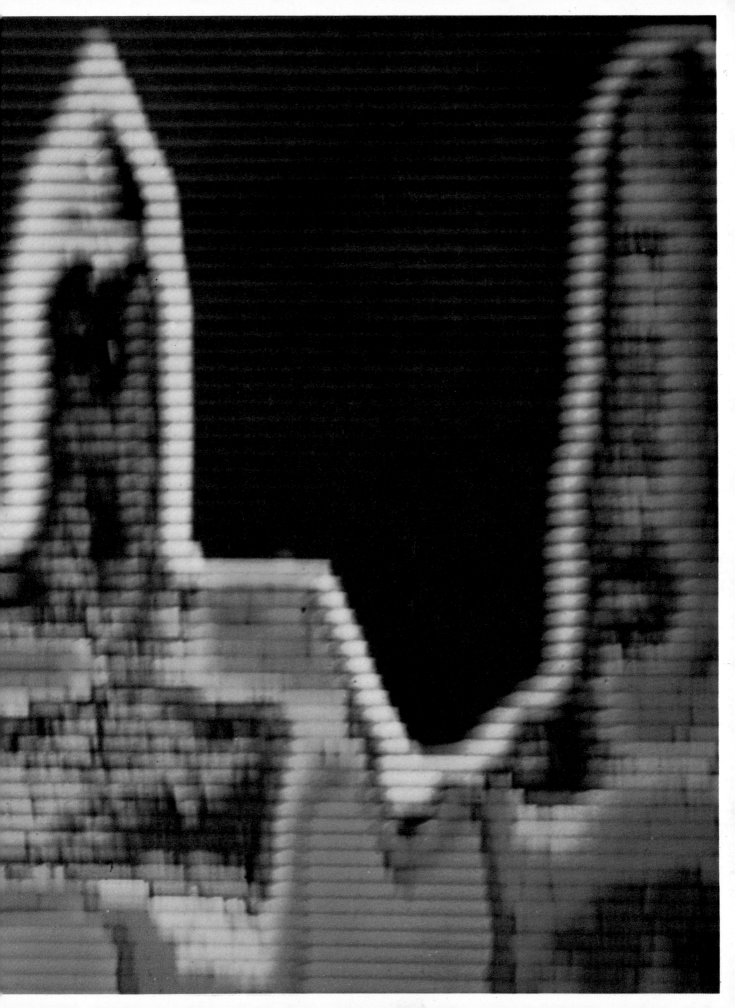

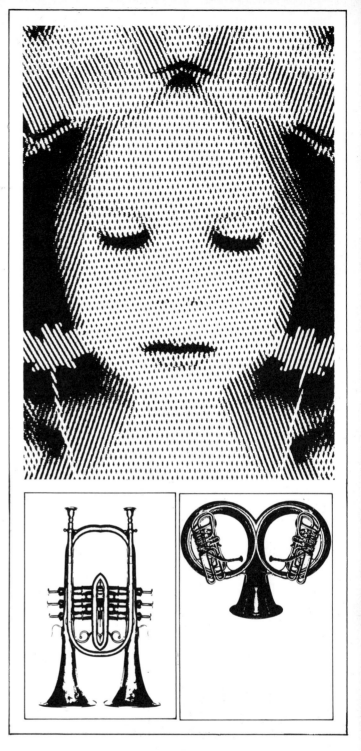

Left **Superb printing technique gives a
remarkably graphic yet fragile quality to
a magnificent Rotterdam snow scene:
photographic composition by C. Gouweleeuw.**
Above **Three impressive examples of the
deceptively simple-looking graphic technique
employed by Belgian photographer
H. Grooteclaes. Sometimes, his otherwise stark
pictures have added colour in selected areas,
other parts of the print having been masked
with special solution before the photograph is
bathed in suitable water-colour dye.**

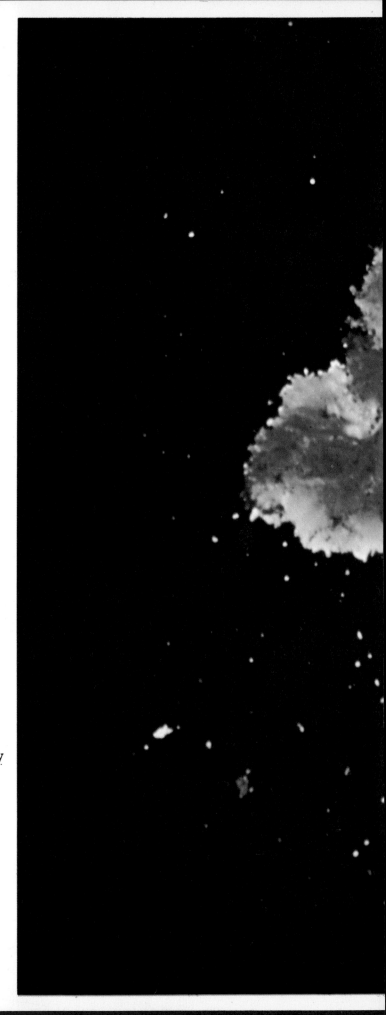

Using a variety of techniques and equipment, photographers have been able to produce many remarkable pictures illustrating the wonders and workings of the human body — but none quite so moving or as beautiful as this 11-week old human foetus with placenta, embryonic sac and forming facial features clearly visible. Swedish photographer Lennart Nilsson, also famous for his endoscopic photography revealing the inner secrets of the heart, worked closely with doctors and obstetricians in producing this picture — one of a history-making series depicting life as it is within the womb.

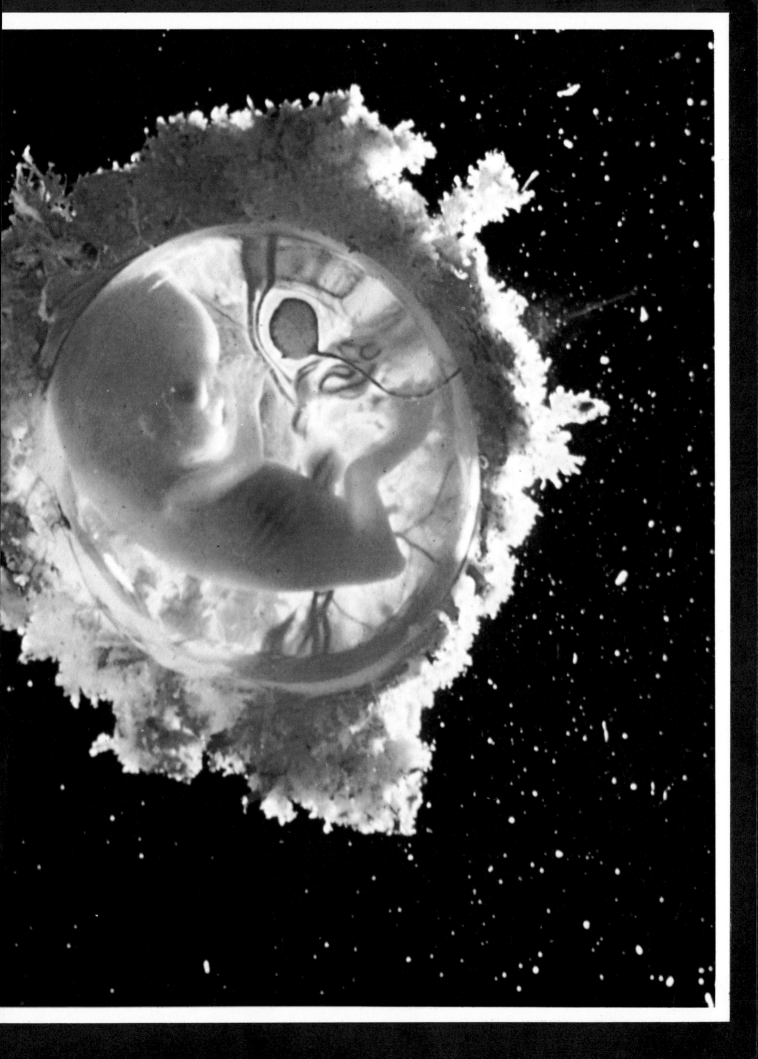

Flashbacks

Photography was born in 1725 when an obscure German professor by the name of Johann Schulze noticed that a glass jar of chemical salts which he had been mixing had changed colour on one side — the side that faced an open window.

Scientists at that time believed that chemicals changed colour only from exposure to heat or air. Schulze realized that they had been wrong all the time. Neither heat nor air was responsible in this case. It was light!

To prove his deduction, he filled another jar with a similar mixture and pasted some stencils on to the outside. He stood it on a window ledge until the chemicals had turned deep purple, then removed the stencils — they had left a clear white image in the salts. Although Johann Schulze did not know it at the time, his discovery was the breakthrough that was to make photography possible.

The optical principle of the camera had been known for centuries. The ancient Greeks knew that light shining through a small hole in the wall of a darkened room would project an inverted image of the view outside on to the opposite wall. The Latin name for this was *camera obscura*. All that prevented them from taking pictures with a *camera obscura* was a means of fixing the image so that it did not disappear when the sun went down.

The discovery that light darkened some chemicals made this possible, although it was not until 100 years after Professor Schulze had published his observations that the first photograph was taken.

The first attempts at photography were made in 1802 by Thomas Wedgwood, an amateur scientist, and his friend Sir Humphrey Davy. Using white paper or white leather coated with a solution of silver nitrate, they were able to make copies of leaves, insects' wings and paintings on glass, but they did not discover a method of fixing the image and so could only view the fruits of their labours by discreet candlelight. If they admired their handiwork for too long, they found that the whole picture darkened, so there was little opportunity to exhibit their achievements.

A few years later, a retired French army officer named Joseph Nicéphore Niépce began experimenting with different light-sensitive materials and in 1826, after much trial and error, he took the first successful photograph — a view from the workroom window of his home near Chalon-sur-Saône.

He did it with a simple camera made for him by a Paris optician and a pewter plate coated with bitumen of Judea dissolved in oil of lavender. He had discovered that the coating hardened when exposed to light. So after an eight hour exposure he used a solvent to wash away the soft areas of the coating and the result was a permanent positive picture — a bleary view of a pigeon house, the roof of a barn and a pear tree with a patch of sky showing through the branches.

Niépce was a taciturn, cautious man and, while he was delighted to let the world know he had taken a photograph, he was unwilling to share the secret of his success. However, in 1829 he was persuaded to sign a partnership agreement with Louis Daguerre, a theatrical designer who had made an improved type of *camera obscura*.

Four years later Niépce died, but Daguerre continued experimenting and by 1837 he had perfected a method of developing photographic plates by mercury vapour, which brought down the exposure time from eight hours to a matter of 20 minutes, and had discovered a way of fixing the pictures with a solution of common salt. Without much thought for his late partner, he named the invention the Daguerrotype.

'Painting is Dead'

On 19th August, 1839, details of the process were made public. The news was greeted with a wave of excitement that swept through Paris. Within an hour, opticians' shops throughout the city were jammed with people clamouring to buy the equipment. The very idea that it was possible to make an exact, true to life reproduction of Nature on a piece of metal astounded and delighted the public. 'From today,' the painter Paul Delaroche exclaimed in some bewilderment, 'painting is dead.'

Not everyone was as enthusiastic about the inven-

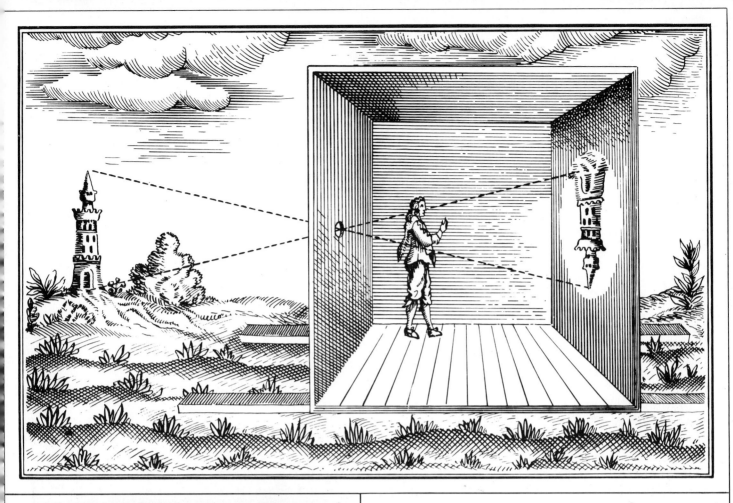

Aristotle first described the basic optical principles of the camera obscura, as shown *above*. But not until the early 1800s did anyone manage to record such images with chemicals. In 1826, Nicéphore Niépce produced the first known photograph on a pewter plate — the view from his window *left*. Fortunately, prints survive too of his only glass negative *below left*. The earliest daguerrotype showing a corner of Daguerre's own studio *below right*.

A common complaint about the early daguerrotypes was that they looked austere: that the images lacked heart and tone. Soon, however, a method of hand-colouring was invented, and the family group *right*, dating from around 1857, is by Antoine Claudet who produced some of the most effective colour pictures of the period. First the outline would be traced on to glass, and stencils would be made for each colour. Using a camel-hair brush with feather-light touch, he would then place finely powdered colour with gum arabic mixture on to the photograph's surface. Such retouching was hardly realistic and an enormous amount of detail, background particularly, was very commonly painted in. Yet within a few years, colour pictures of exceptionally good quality were being taken. *Below* Car and costumes set the period as early this century in a charming example of

an autochrome — the first really effective, practical and popular colour process invented by the Lumiere brothers of Lyons who used tiny grains of starch dyed red, green and blue to cover the photographic plate. The process itself was really a very slow one by today's standards: and subjects such as the endearing young girl photographed by the sea *below* may have had to pose for this autochrome for as long as two minutes.

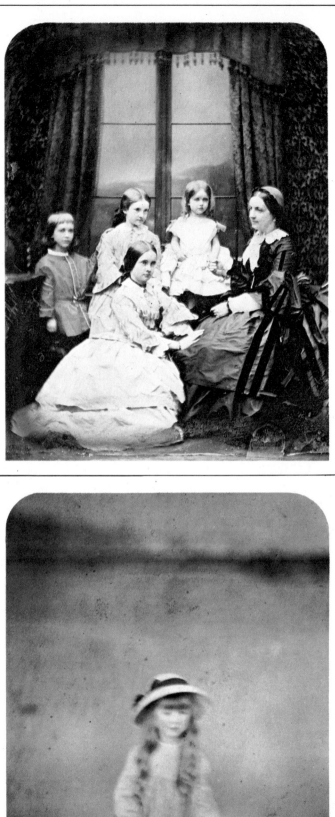

ART-PROGRESS.

Artist (!). "NOW, MUM! TAKE ORF YER 'EAD FOR SIXPENCE, OR YER 'OLE BODY FOR A SHILLIN'!"

tion and in some reactionary circles the Daguerrotype was condemned on religious grounds. A German newspaper commented bitterly: 'The wish to capture evanescent reflections is not only impossible, as has been shown by thorough German investigation, but the mere desire alone, the will to do so, is blasphemy. God created man in His own image, and no man-made machine may fix the image of God . . .'

Blasphemy or no, there was no denying that photography had arrived. With the announcement of Daguerre's process, dozens of other inventors working on similar lines came forward with claims that they, too, had produced pictures by light. But none of them produced a process comparable to the Daguerrotype.

Although they had many disadvantages, the quality of the Daguerrotypes was astonishing — they had brilliant clarity and detail that is difficult to surpass, even today.

The only serious rival was a process called the Calotype, invented by William Henry Fox Talbot, an aristocratic Englishman, who had managed to make permanent photographic images on paper. He eventually perfected a negative-positive technique on which modern photography was later to be based, but the pictures were rather soft and, although a number of prints could be taken from one negative, they were considered generally inferior to the Daguerrotype.

The demand for photography increased so rapidly that in 1849 some 10,000 Parisians had themselves daguerrotyped, provoking harsh criticism from the poet Charles Baudelaire, who deplored 'our squalid society that rushed, Narcissus to a man, to gaze at its trivial image on a scrap of metal.' By the 1850s more than three million Daguerrotypes had been produced in America alone and in England the University of London added photography to its curriculum.

The Two-Second 'Snap'

In 1851 photography entered a new era with the invention by Frederick Scott Archer, an Englishman, of the 'wet collodion process'. Collodion was a viscous liquid which could be spread on glass and coated with light-sensitive chemicals. This gave greatly increased sensitivity and consequently sharper pictures, and, more important, it enabled exposures to be reduced to as little as two seconds. With this new process, photographers could point their cameras at almost any subject and expect a reasonable result.

The amount of equipment needed by an early photographer using the wet collodion process was enormous. In addition to a camera and tripod and several lenses, he needed a case full of chemicals, a supply of glass plates, dishes, scales, glass measures and funnels, a pail of rinsing water and a darkroom where the processing could be carried out.

Portraiture was the staple business of the first professional photographers and in all the major cities of the world the competition for business was intense. In 1857 the English magazine *Punch* published a cartoon showing four photographers touting for business from a woman passer-by. One of them is saying: 'Now, Mum! Take off yer 'ead for sixpence, or yer 'ole body for a shillin'!'

Realizing the demand, a Parisian photographer called André Disdéri devised a practical way of reducing production costs by taking eight portraits on one plate — a forerunner of the famous Polyphoto multiple photograph.

Disdéri's idea led to a craze for *carte-de-visite* photographs and he became so famous that in May 1859, when Napoleon III was marching out of Paris at the head of his army en route to Italy, the Emperor halted his troops in the Boulevard des Italiens and went into Disdéri's studio to have his picture taken. All fashionable Paris followed the Emperor's example and by 1861 Disdéri was reputed to be the richest photographer in the world, grossing £48,000 a year from his Paris studio alone.

Sadly his business acumen did not match his flair for showmanship and he died penniless in a public hospital in Nice. In part he was the victim of his own invention — the process he popularized was so easy to imitate that *cartes-de-visite* could be produced by almost anyone.

Enthusiastic Amateurs

After the 1850s more and more amateurs took up photography, apparently undeterred by the huge amount of equipment needed. As enlargement was not yet possible, cameras tended to be comparatively large in order to produce big and impressive pictures. It was common for a photographer to carry about with him a 20 by 16 inch plate camera.

In 1860 a keen Glasgow amateur by the name of John Kibble had a camera made for him, so large that it had to be mounted on wheels and drawn by a horse. The glass plates measured 44 by 36 inches and each one weighed more than 40 pounds. Mr Kibble built greenhouses for a living, so the immense glass plates were no problem to him.

By the 1870s the lot of both amateur and professional photographer was improved with the gradual introduction of mass-produced photographic material, in particular plates ready coated with dry gelatine. This freed photographers from the necessity of having to prepare their own plates with wet collodion. Within a decade their load was made even lighter by the invention of celluloid film.

In the light of the difficulties created by cumbersome equipment and complicated technical processes, the artistic and technical achievements of the early photographers are awesome. They explored the aesthetic potential of the medium with the same imagination and diligence that they applied to solving its technical problems and during the first two decades of photography, they had tackled every possible type of picture, from reportage to landscapes, from still life to action

Typical of the pioneers of those early days was Auguste Bisson, a successful Paris photographer. In 1861 he decided to take some pictures from the summit of Mont Blanc in the Alps. It took 25 porters three days to carry his cameras, tripods, glass plates, chemicals, developing tent and other equipment up the 16,000 foot mountain. Once there, despite exhaustion and the biting cold, Bisson managed to expose three plates and develop them in his tent. He used snow melted by the feeble heat of an oil lamp to rinse the plates.

Three years later an English photographer, Samuel Bourne, made a ten-week tour of the Himalayas and several other expeditions, one lasting as long as nine months and requiring 60 porters to carry his equipment. The pictures taken by men like Bisson and Bourne captivated the public — it was their first sight of remote regions of the world which had just been names on a map.

Photographers were quick to realize the power of the camera in the field of social documentation. Between 1887 and 1892, Jacob Riis, a police court reporter for *The New York Tribune*, took a series of photographs which highlighted the plight of the poor in America and so awakened the public conscience that the Governor of New York State instituted a number of social reforms as a direct result.

So much was achieved so quickly in the early development of photography that, sadly, many of the achievements went unrecognized. Thousands of pictures that today provide us with a unique insight into life a century or more ago were taken by unknown amateur photographers. They were not to know that their pictures would be riveting in 100 years' time.

The scandalized reaction of that German newspaper to the invention of the Daguerrotype seems very curious now, in the light of the benefits that photography has brought to the world. This is how the editorial ended: 'Is it possible that God should have abandoned His eternal principles, and allowed a Frenchman in Paris to give the world an invention of the Devil . . . If this thing were at all possible, then something similar would have been done a long time ago in antiquity by men like Archimedes or Moses. But if these wise men knew nothing of mirror pictures made permanent, then one can straightway call the Frenchman Daguerre, who boasts of such unheard of things, the fool of fools.'

Subtle in tone and composition, both the photographs opposite were taken early this century and perhaps not surprisingly bear a remarkable resemblance to contemporary Impressionist paintings. Colour had come a long way since Maxwell's first attempts at reproducing a tartan ribbon using three separate black and white photographs taken with different filters: red, green and blue. Having one's portrait taken during these early years was very much the fashionable thing, and an enormous amount of complicated, lethal-looking equipment would be used lest the subject move before that vital 'click'. Particularly fascinating, too, for the Victorians was another newly-developed technique: paired prints which, when viewed through a stereoscope, gave a startling effect of relief or 3-D. Style was becoming less static: pictures were about to come to life.

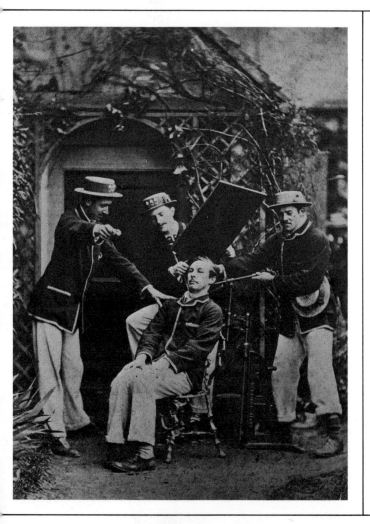

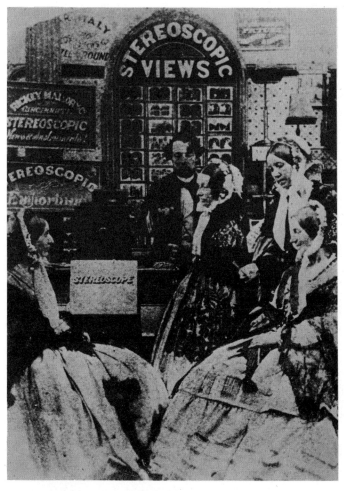

Top left **A daguerrotype view of the Pont Neuf in Paris, 1842. Exposure time for very early daguerrotypes could be anything up to 30 minutes at times. So it was not until Daguerre (depicted above discovering the sensitivity of light to silver iodine) had perfected his process that daguerrotypes were widely used for portraiture. But the silver-** **toned daguerrotype was expensive: delicate too. Englishman William Henry Fox Talbot** *top right* **had worked for some time at improving his photogenic drawings: the result an impressively effective, far more economical process known first as the calotype, later the talbotype. This was photography on paper, and two highly graphic examples of the**

very same picture, positive and negative, are shown. First the paper would be carefully coated in silver nitrate and potassium iodide. Washed in gallic acid and silver nitrate, it became even more sensitive to light. Once exposed, the paper was coated yet again in similar solution to develop the image. Within minutes of heating, the negative pic-ture was formed. It would then have to be fixed with potassium bromide (later hyposulphite of soda) before a positive print could be made. On this page *above* a calotype of Hungerford Bridge, also by Fox Talbot: *below* the Bridge at Orleans, a print from *The Pencil of Nature,* Talbot's own publication on the beginnings of photography, dated 1844.

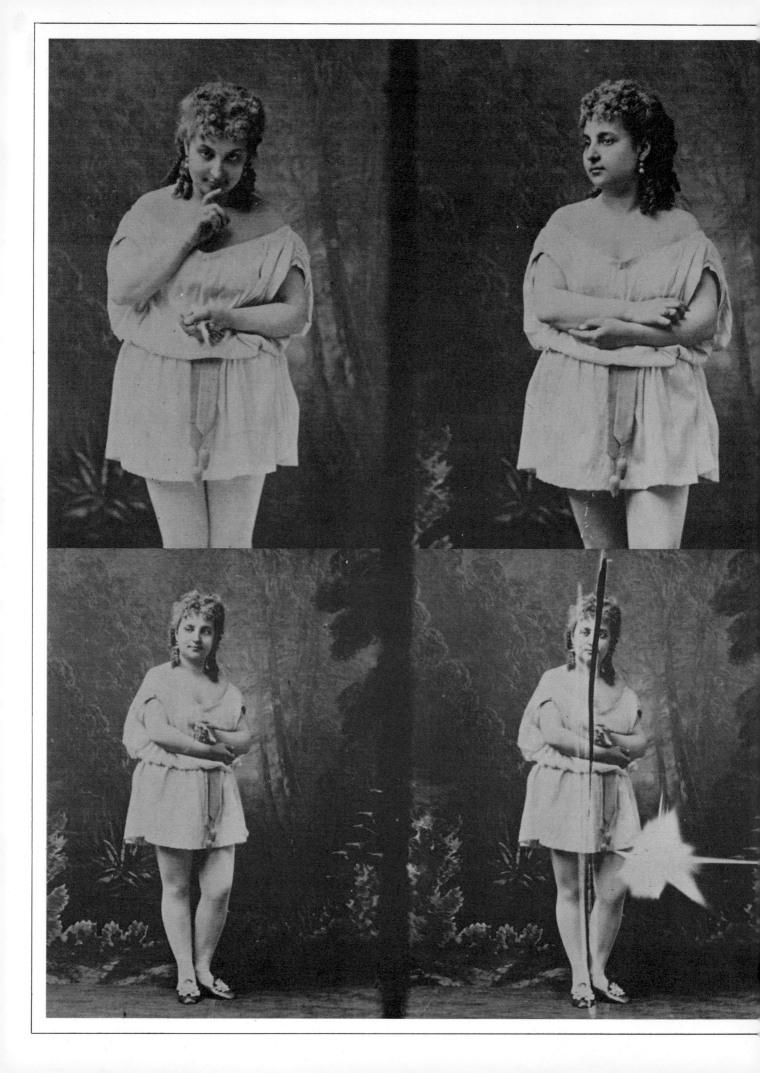

With the carte-de-visite process, patented in 1854 by Disderi, several photographs could be produced on one negative — final prints looking much like today's popular Polyphotos. *Left* An amusing set of Disderi cartes-de-visite of a dancing girl. *Above* One of a similar set showing '*Skittles*' Walters: *below* General and Mrs Tom Thumb.

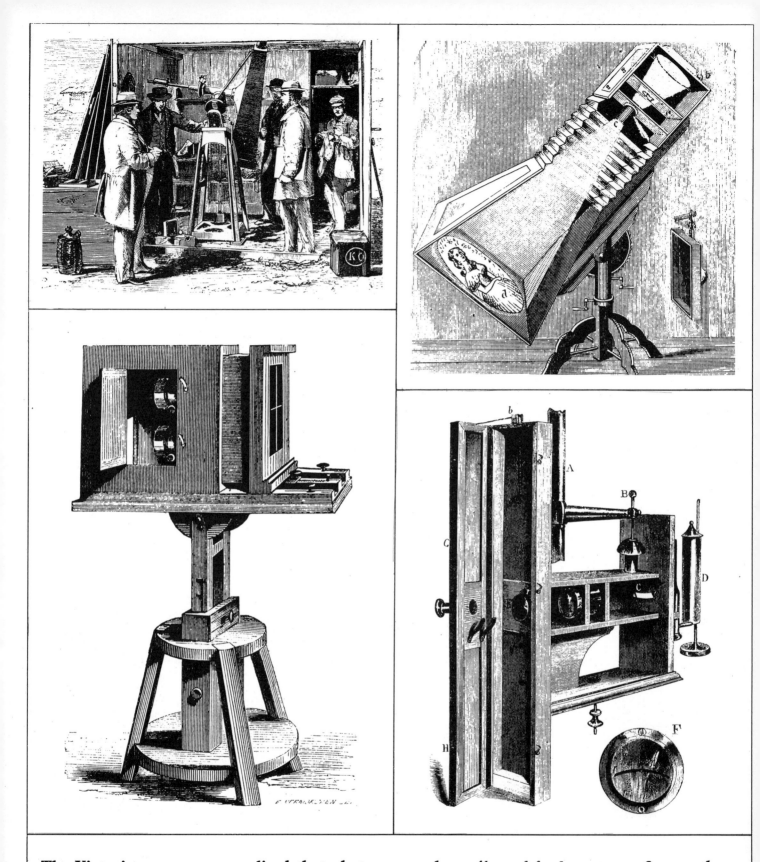

The Victorians very soon realized that photography was not only an art form and means of reportage. Scope was far wider. It could also be used to further scientific analysis and discovery. *Top left* On 18th July 1860, Warren De La Rue took the world's first successful picture of a total eclipse. Equipment and techniques were quickly becoming complex. *Above left* A camera for producing visiting cards which took four pictures at once, for economy's sake. *Top right* Special apparatus for making enlargements using sunlight. *Above* An even more intricate camera designed, according to Louis Figuier's *Les Merveilles de La Science* of 1870 'for photographing changes in the electrification of air

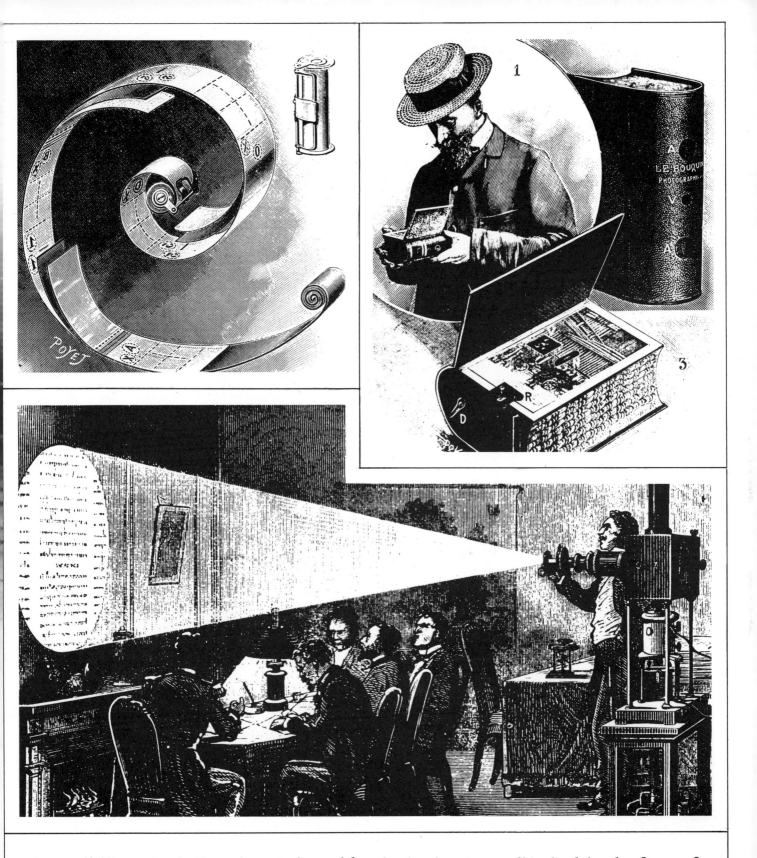

using a 'falling plate'. Experimentation with various forms of plate and film were continually being made and by 1904, photographers were already envisaging a form of roll film on which each separate negative could be removed for processing when desired, as shown in this engraving from the French publication *La Nature*. Possibilities seemed endless: even the 'spy' camera, disguised in the form of a book, was now perfectly feasible; and microphotographs containing minute secret messages are thought to have been sent out by carrier pigeon during the Siege of Paris in the Franco-Prussian War in 1870-1. The microphotographs could be projected onto a wall and read on arrival.

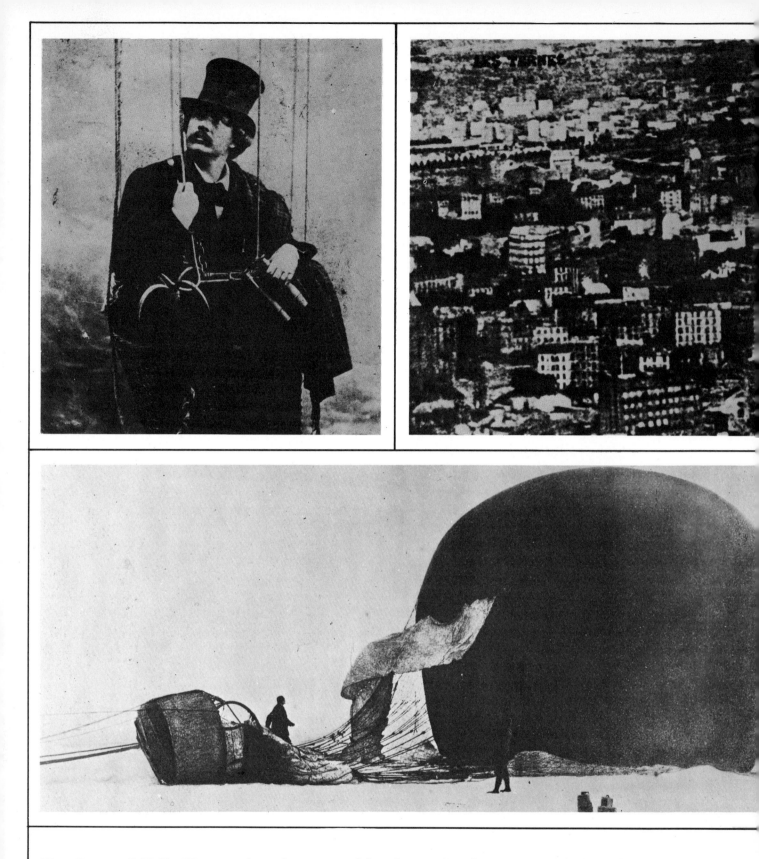

Top **Gaspard Felix Tournachon, known to his public as Nadar, was famed not only as a balloonist. He was also the Frenchman who claimed personally to have raised both metaphorically and literally the science of photography to the height of art! His brilliant portraiture, featured later in this book, was outstanding for the period: while in 1858** he took what was probably the world's first aerial photograph — a view of Paris from an altitude of 520 metres. This was an age of discovery, and photography was certainly going places. *Above* **The balloon in which a photographer and his party of explorers had attempted to reach the North Pole in 1897. What makes this early picture even more**

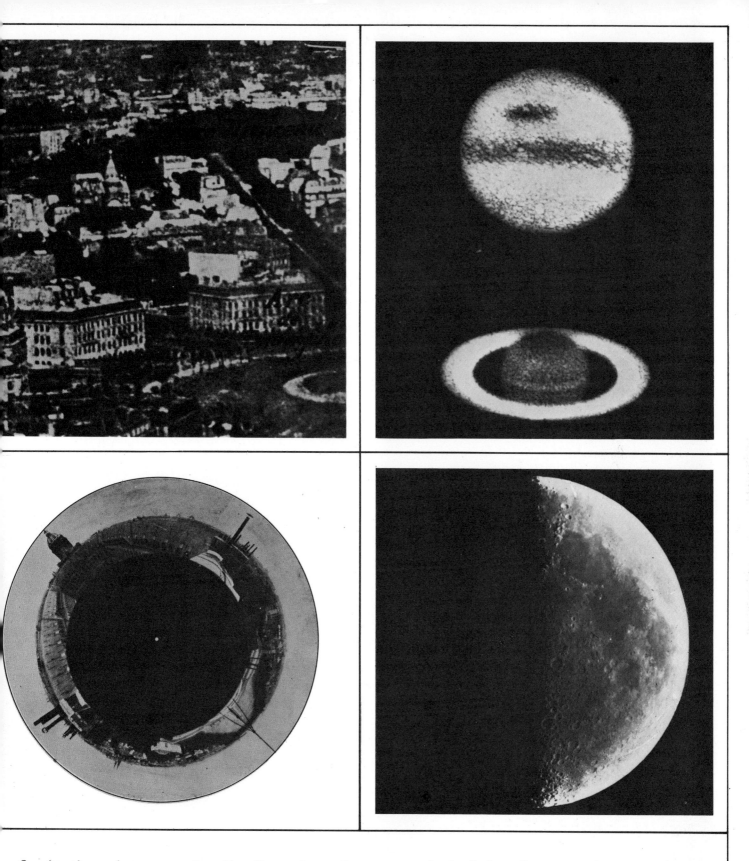

fascinating, however, is the fact that the exposed film was not discovered and finally processed until 33 years after the balloon had crashed in Polar ice. *Above* An unusual early view of Paris with almost fisheye effect. By now, photography was also being used for permanent recording of the planets. *Top* Jupiter and Saturn taken by A. A. Common in 1879 and 1885 respectively: below these two pictures, remarkable for their date, a highly detailed photograph of the moon's mysterious pitted surface taken 1877 in a last quarter. Still a comparatively recent invention, the new world of photography was already proving itself an indispensable aid to exploration and investigation, on earth and beyond.

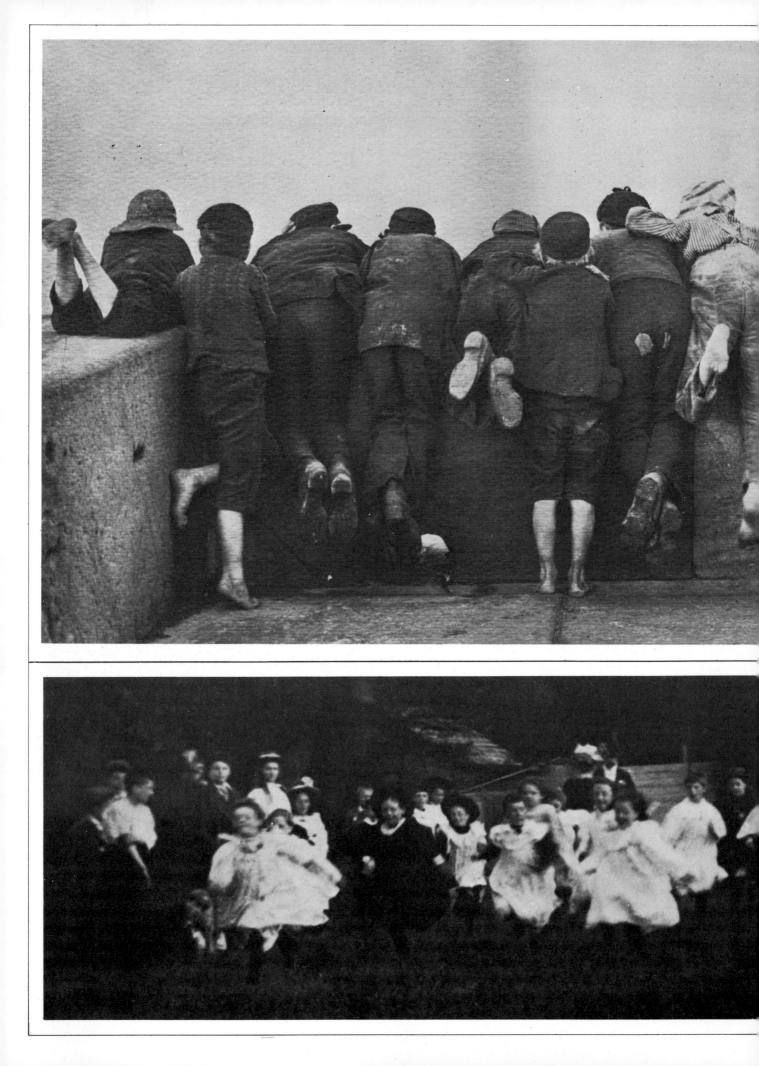

A spread of early photographs of children, seen both formally and at play. *Opposite* The boys in Sutcliff's *Stern Realities* intriguingly peer over an old stone wall: and G. Wilkes records an exhilarating race over open fields. *Top* Gertrude Käsebier, one of the American school of Photo-Secession, uses impressionistic effects in her picture of a dancing class.

Not unexpectedly, the camera was soon to become a vital tool for the traveller, providing as it did an accurate recording of the scenery, peoples and customs of other countries. Well before 1900, photographers were considered essential to expeditions to the unknown: and this in spite of the fact that scores of additional porters and carriers must have been necessary merely to carry all the equipment. Samuel Bourne, an English photographer, is renowned for his expedition to the Himalayas. In a most attractive collection of pictures, he revealed to an untravelled outside world the almost ethereal beauty of the Indian peoples, their mountains and countryside. *Below* A village scene in southern India: and *bottom* a Darjeeling group of Bhotias. How startled these peoples must have been by the cameras,

we can only conjecture. Jacob Riis, reporter on the New York Herald Tribune at the end of the last century, was one of the first to use photography as a pointer to the need for social reform. In a poignant series, published as a book entitled *How The Other Half Lives,* he recorded, for more cushioned sections of society, the appalling and shameful slum conditions of the American poor. *Below* We, too, almost a hundred years later, enter one of the very dark alleys of 19th century America's many poverty stricken quarters. Riis depicts the sordidness with accuracy: but always in his pictures one can sense his marked affection for those for whom such tenement buildings were home. *Left* Riis captures the tender expressions of children at prayer in a state-run orphanage.

The Portrait

The American photographer Bert Stern once explained that the Chinese dislike being photographed because they believe that a part of their life is then being taken away. 'And in a way,' he said, 'they're right.' The attempt to remove part of the sitter's life, or at least to expose it, is the ultimate goal of the portrait photographer.

A portrait must show more than just a face; it should capture something of the character, strength and personality of the sitter. In the search for this quality, the importance of the actual features can become secondary — indeed some of the most powerful photographic portraits ever taken do not even show the full face.

Karsh of Ottawa, one of the most famous modern portrait photographers, did not agree with this view. Most of his pictures are in the simple head-and-shoulders format, but what distinguishes them as outstanding portraits is the dignity and strength that they reveal.

All his life he was obsessed by a desire to expose the 'inner power' which he believed great men and women possess. He was more interested in the mind and soul of his sitters than in their appearance. It was the function of the photographer, he said, to recognize the moment at which the sitter revealed his or her greatness. It could be reflected through eyes, hands or attitude and might only last a split second — but that was the moment to take the picture.

During his career, Karsh became so famous that to have a portrait taken by him was almost a symbol of success; among the many famous people who posed for his camera were six American presidents, three popes and most of the world's greatest painters, writers and musicians.

Part of the secret of his success was that he exercised total control over his sitter. No matter who entered his studio in Ottawa, when the session began only one man — Karsh — was in charge. He dressed the Russian statesman Khrushchev in a massive fur coat and woollen Balaclava helmet for his portrait; he made the painter Miro change from a formal suit into everyday working clothes; and when, in 1941, Winston Churchill refused to remove his cigar for a picture, Karsh coolly plucked it from his lips. His portrait of Churchill was perhaps the most famous picture he ever took: the bulldog determination and power of the great wartime leader was perfectly captured.

Most portrait photographers try to create an identifiable style of their own, so that no matter who is being photographed the man behind the camera will also be recognized. Latvian-born Philippe Halsman is an exception. The work of this extraordinarily versatile photographer ranges from sombre, serious portraits to slapstick humour and to strange surrealism.

The producer of more than 100 *Life* magazine cover pictures, Halsman has taken literally thou-

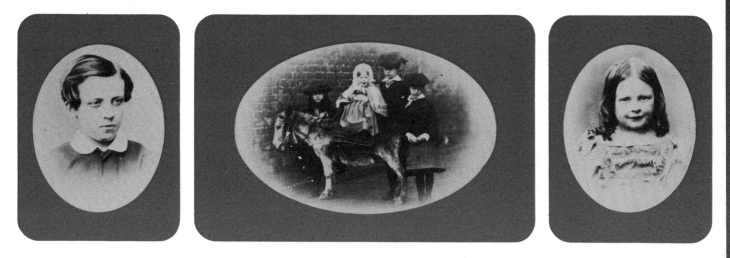

sands of portraits. His aim, when photographing famous people, has always been to produce a definitive image of that person — he has succeeded on many occasions, notably with his forceful picture of Albert Einstein in 1948. The straggly white hair, the lined forehead, penetrating eyes, and mouth concealed behind an untidy moustache — the way Halsman saw Einstein is the way he is remembered in history. That picture, and one of Adlai Stevenson, was used on US postage stamps.

Halsman has taken many pictures of the surrealist painter Salvador Dali including 36 completely different views of his famous moustache! One of his most masterly pictures of the artist is as surreal as any of Dali's paintings — he posed seven nude models to simulate a skull and photographed the painter in top hat and white tie beside them. Halsman's *Jump Book* was an excursion in a quite different direction: it comprised portraits of 177 people all jumping into the air with absurd abandon.

The Serious Early Days

Such an idea was unheard of in the early days of photography, when portraiture was a serious business. The subjects had to sit or stand absolutely still, and to assist them their heads were often fixed into specially constructed clamps. They were usually posed in front of backdrops of crudely-painted allegorical scenes and it seemed a require-

The human face was not unexpectedly among the camera's first subjects. Some charming early vignettes by Henry Peach Robinson, later known for his art-photography.

ment of the Victorian era that they should glare into the camera as miserably as possible.

The proliferation of photographic studios (in London alone there were more than 200 by 1861) and the development of cheap *cartes-de-visite* portraits did not, predictably, please the portrait painters. However, many of them believed that they had an unbeatable advantage over 'upstart' photographers. As a court painter replied, when Queen Victoria asked him if he was not afraid that photography would ruin his livelihood: 'Ah no, Madame. Photography can't flatter!'

Nevertheless, the public demand for photographic portraits literally swept the Western world. While most of the *cartes-de-visite* pictures made little contribution to the photographic art, a number of the less commercially-minded photographers were taking superb portraits, notably Nadar, Etienne Carjat and Julia Margaret Cameron. It was the work of such photographers which gave the majority of the public their first idea of what the celebrities of the day actually looked like.

Mrs Cameron was an extraordinary person. She took up photography merely for amusement in middle age, but was soon describing it as a 'divine art'. With remarkable vision, she declared her aim was to record 'the greatness of the inner, as well as the features of the outer, man' and to this end she pioneered a totally new portraiture technique — the close-up. As well as photographing many of the great Victorians — among them Tennyson, Browning and Darwin — she also recruited friends, family and servants to sit for her. The striking picture she took of Sir John Herschel in 1867 is still regarded as one of the finest photographic portraits ever taken.

Lewis Carroll, author of *Alice in Wonderland*, was also a keen amateur photographer and his best pictures were casual and charming portraits of little girls. Small boys did not figure in his repertoire — 'I am fond of children,' he once said, 'except boys.'

By the turn of the century portrait photographers were experimenting with new ways of capturing the character of their subjects. Alvin Langdon Coburn first came to prominence with a portrait of George Bernard Shaw which the writer liked so much that he described Coburn as 'one of the most accomplished and sensitive artist photographers now living'. After such lavish praise almost inevitably he became famous, mainly as a photographer of leading writers and painters. But his abstract portraits, much influenced by Cubist painters, really broke new ground — he devised a lens attachment to produce multiple-image pictures and using this technique took many innovative pictures. One of the most successful was a portrait of the poet Ezra Pound.

Experiments of this kind set all branches of photography free. The aspirations of the portrait photographer had not changed since they were defined by Julia Margaret Cameron fifty years earlier, but a new attitude emerged: in the endless search for soul and character, any approach was possible.

Edward Steichen, a brilliant American photographer of the 1920s and 30s, was quick to appreciate the infinite potential of the camera in portraiture. As early as 1902 he produced an imaginative study of the sculptor Rodin with two of his most famous works, using two negatives. More than 30 years later, he was still taking strikingly original portraits — his photograph of the writer Carl Sandburg comprised six profiles, all shot in one session, giving an extraordinary impression of animation.

In England, Angus McBean, best known for his work as a theatrical photographer, was breaking new ground with his attempts to combine surrealistic fantasy and photographic realism. His self-portrait, using a wide angle lens and four exposures, is an astonishing example of the technical possibilities of the camera.

'Candid' portraits

Not all portrait photographers used a studio as their place of work. In 1908 Arthur Barrett took some wonderfully expressive close-ups of suffragettes in the dock at Bow Street Court in London by hiding his camera in his top hat and shooting through a hole cut for the lens. But undoubtedly the pioneer of 'candid' portraiture was Dr Erich Salomon, whose pictures taken during the Coburg murder trial in 1928 with a camera hidden in a briefcase caused a sensation.

Salomon built up such a reputation for candid pictures of celebrities at work, particularly statesmen at international conferences, that it became a standard joke among politicians that no one would believe their meetings were important unless Salomon photographed them. He became so expert at getting into functions at which photographers were normally barred that Aristide Briand, French Minister of Foreign Affairs in the early 1930s, described him as 'le roi des indiscrets' — the king of indiscretion.

Portrait photography has also been used as a form of social documentation. August Sander, a German, devoted his career to photographing all classes of German society from the days of the Kaiser to the beginning of the Second World War. He was interested not in portraits of individuals but of types. Most of his sitters were formally posed and shown staring straight ahead, yet the collection of pictures he compiled gives an insight into life in pre-war Germany far more revealing than many techniques of pure photo-journalism. Because his portfolio showed ordinary folk without any attempt at idealization and because a number of them were Jews, the Gestapo confiscated it in 1934, but he hid all the negatives for more than ten years — and saved for history a unique record of German society during those calamitous years.

Artists and the camera

The portrait photographer's most challenging problem — to reveal the 'inner man' — is most severely tested when the sitters are themselves artists, for in this confrontation the camera is competing on equal terms with art. Arnold Newman, an American, met the challenge by photographing artists in poses and settings suggestive of their work. He composes his portraits with infinite care and skill, treating the subject as only one element of the final picture. What he aims to achieve with every

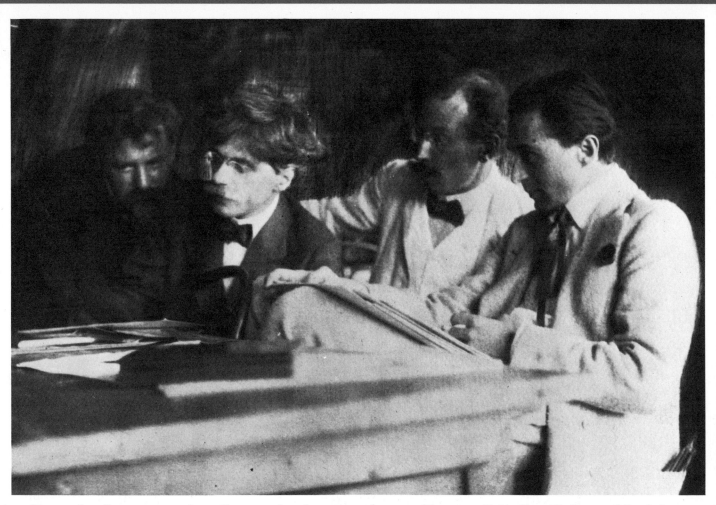

Portrait of concentration: four early photographers — Eugene, Stieglitz, Kuhn and Steichen

portrait is a permanent work of photographic art, able to stand on its own merits as durably as any painting in a museum.

To this end he will bully or cajole the sitter into position and wait for hours, if necessary, for the right expression. After exposing his pictures, he makes dozens of prints until he has achieved a satisfactory balance of contrast and composition.

Newman's work is very much a product of the early avant-garde photographers who were willing to experiment and explore every by-way of the medium. His portrait of the Israeli painter and sculptor, Yaacov Agam, for example, was created by cutting a slice off the side of one print, tearing the remainder in half then laying the three pieces on top of an identical print and re-photographing it. The result is powerfully reminiscent of Agam's kinetic works of art.

In the hands of an imaginative and innovative photographer, the camera's potential in terms of portraiture seems almost limitless. Duane Michals, an American, believes that a good photographic portrait need not necessarily show even the features of the subject; he is more concerned with creating what he calls a 'visual image' of the sitter's per-

sonality. His portrait of the Belgian surrealist painter René Magritte is a classic example. With the help of a double exposure, the shadowy figure of Magritte is seen superimposed over an empty canvas on an easel in front of a window. On the left hand side of the picture, a second image of the painter is reflected in a mirror. It captures perfectly Magritte's distinctive style.

Sometimes it has seemed that portrait photography could progress no further, that all combinations of techniques and styles had been exhausted. But in 1959 a book appeared which proved conclusively that the end will never come. Entitled *Observations*, it was a collection of portraits by the American photographer Richard Avedon. The sitters were mainly famous people, but despite the fact that their faces were so well known there was something in each picture that was fresh and quite different. It was as if only one side of them had been seen before and Avedon had photographed them all from the other side. He explained this phenomenon quite simply: 'They are all pictures of me, of the way I feel about the people I photograph.'

So as long as there are new portrait photographers, there will be new photographic portraits.

Nadar's studio, opened in 1853 in the Boulevard des Capucines, Paris, was soon to be frequented by all the great men of Europe — statesmen, artists and scientists alike. The photographer's tremendous flair for publicity and fame as a balloonist, as well as his tremendous talent for portraiture, had brought his name to the fore. *Far left* Victor Hugo: and on this page, *top left* Offenbach, *below left* Baudelaire and *below* Liszt. Only very rarely did Nadar choose to photograph a female subject: most of his portraits are of men, celebrities at that, and the most usual composition was a three-quarters length shot. His technique — the collodion process.

Nadar was also renowned for experimental photography. He took the world's first underground pictures in the sewers of Paris and also the very first aerial shots. After a period of pre-occupation with ballooning, Nadar then chose to concentrate again on portraiture, mainly for reasons of finance. But progress had been fast during his absence and he now found himself faced with considerable competition. As he wrote in his autobiography: 'The appearance of Disdéri and the carte-de-visite spelled disaster.' Styles had now changed and his work was no longer as popular. Never again was Nadar to match his original success.

David Octavius Hill and Robert Adamson were a Scottish team of photographers whose output was prolific. They are most widely renowned for their powerful, well-composed portraits but also produced some charming landscape views of Scotland's coast and the Highlands. Many of their works seem to have been taken indoors: but in fact, since sunlight was required for their calotypes, most were posed on the Edinburgh studio porch with an arrangement of drapes in the background. *Top left* Portrait of Mrs Rigby: and combined portrait of John Henning and A. H. Ritchie. Below these, David Octavius Hill himself and an untitled portrait of a young girl. *Below* Untitled child portrait by Julia Cameron. Turn for more examples of her work.

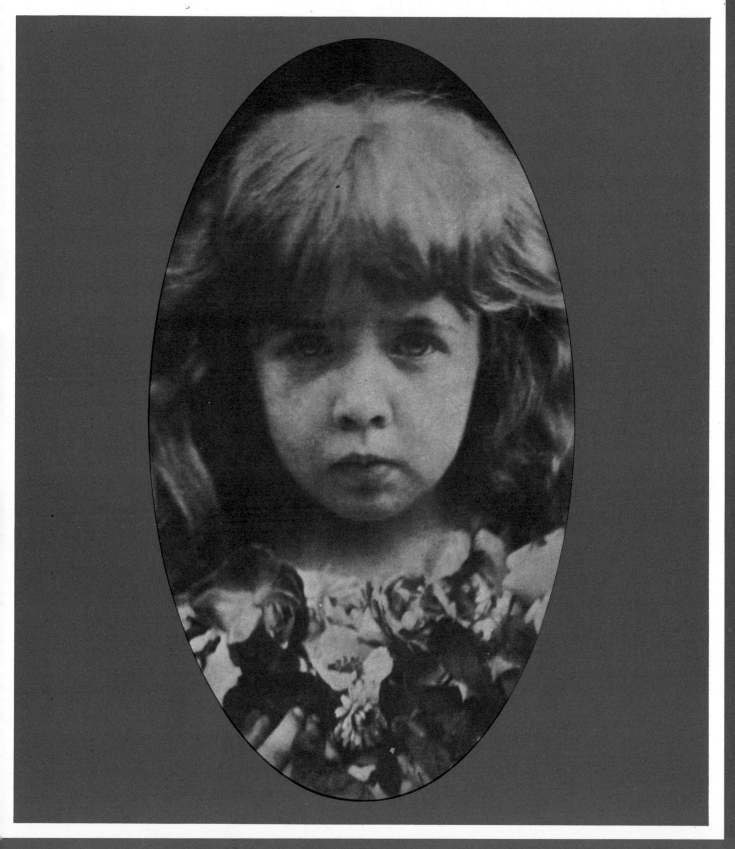

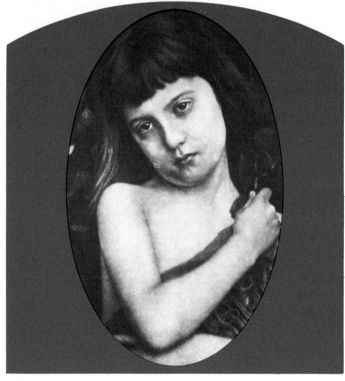

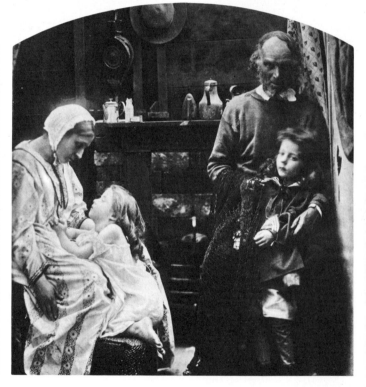

Julia Margaret Cameron did not take up photography until well into middle age and then only as a hobby to start with. Her first successful portrait was taken in 1864, and soon she was to photograph a very large circle of her influential friends — Darwin, Longfellow and Tennyson among them. Her work was not restricted to traditional formal portraits, however. Mrs Cameron's photography always revealed the subject's personality, and she is also renowned for her numerous allegorical portraits, created under the influence of artist George Frederick Watts. *Above left* Mrs. Herbert Duckworth, later Mrs Leslie Stephen and mother of Virginia Woolf, 1867: *above right* a Pre-Raphaelite style photograph May, 1870. *Below* A child as St John The Baptist, 1872: and an allegorical group *Bring Father Safely Home,* about 1872.

The Reverend Charles Dodgson — otherwise Lewis Carroll, author of *Alice in Wonderland*— first took up photography for amusement in the 1850s and is best known both for his portraits of children, particularly the small girls he was so fond of, and also his informal groups. *Above left* One of his earliest known pictures, and below this, Lady Henry Somerset. *Above* Paul Martin's candid portrait of a street urchin, 1898.

Far left **All the characteristic determination of a great political leader captured in this world-famous classical portrait of Sir Winston Churchill, 1941, by Karsh of Ottawa. American photographer Duane Michals believes that to achieve a successful portrait it is not necessary to feature details of facial characteristics: that interpretation of personality is more vital.** *Above* **His bowler-hatted portrait of the surrealist painter Magritte reflected on to a canvas in front of a window, with yet another image reflected to the left in a mirror. Interestingly, Magritte also used mirrors, bowler-hatted men and artists' canvas to produce effects of illusion, mystery and distortion in his paintings.** *Left* **Self-portrait taken with four exposures by Angus McBean, 1946.** *Overleaf* **Portrait of top model Jean Shrimpton by David Bailey. On page 55, portrait of artist Feliks Topolski by Patrick Lichfield, taken with a flash. The swirling effect is in fact a sketch by Topolski drawn with a pencil torch in a darkened room and registering clearly on the film.**

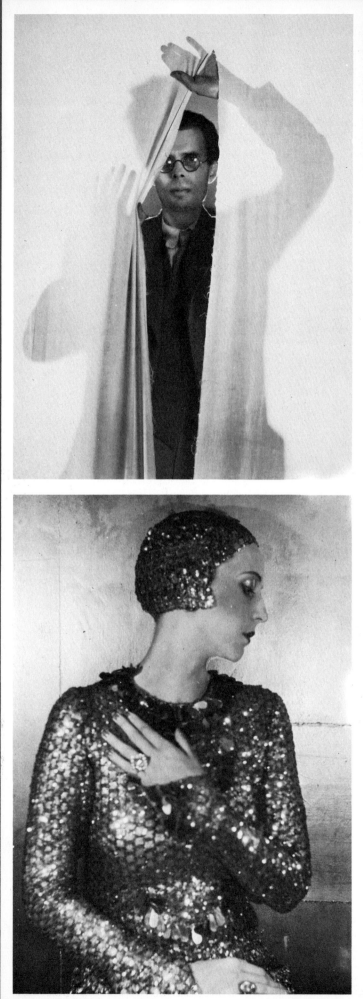

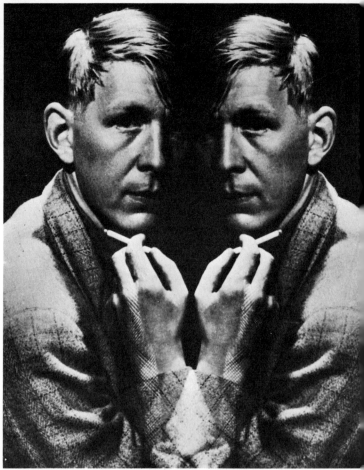

A selection from the outstandingly creative photographic portraiture of Cecil Beaton who was, for some 25 years, principal photographer of both fashion and personalities for *Vogue*. *Above* Aldous Huxley behind a rent curtain, and an intriguing double portrait of poet W. H. Auden. *Left* The glamorous Paula Gellibrand and *below* a sensuous and romantic Marlene Dietrich. *Right* New dimensions to a portrait of playwright Harold Pinter.

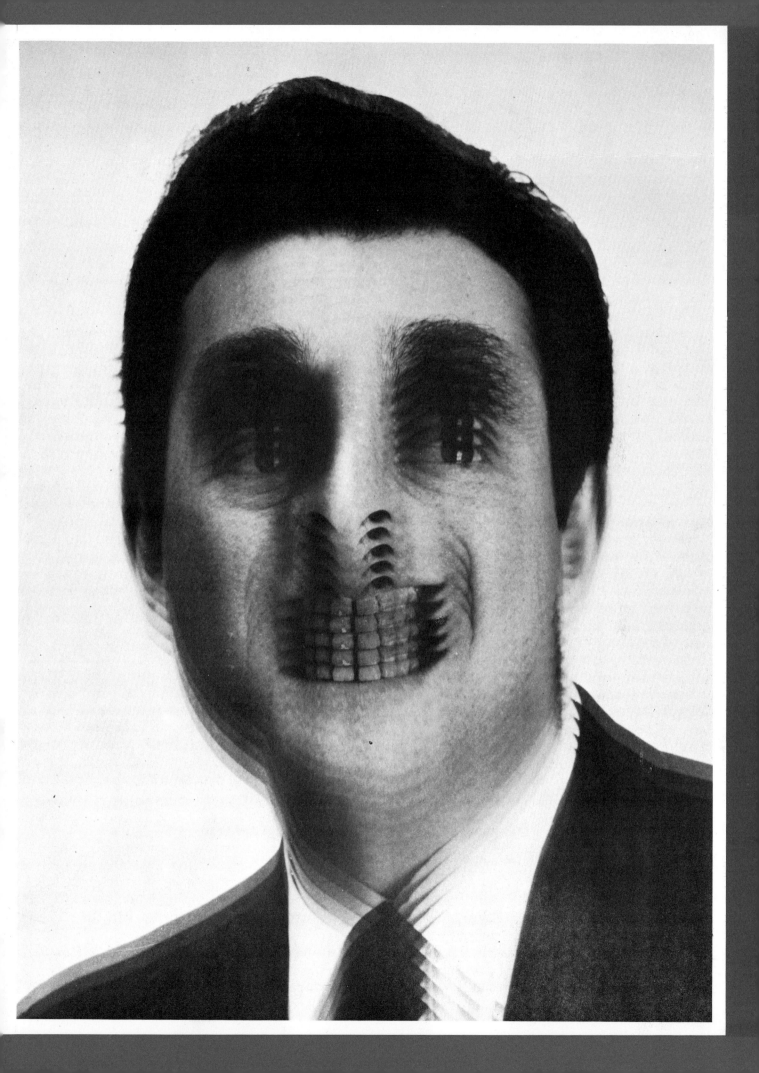

The Concerned Photographer

War; peace; love; hate; poverty; wealth; happiness; sorrow . . . nothing gives us a better view of the human condition than a camera. Its candid eye can record with equal concern the tranquil bliss of motherhood and first love, and the savage hate, fear and squalor of war.

Many photographers have dedicated, indeed still do dedicate, their entire careers to the documentation of our life and times. Some of them are motivated by a social conscience — a desire to expose evil, injustice or inequality with their camera. But mainly they are people who find it impossible not to be involved in the subjects they are photographing; in a slum they may find beauty and in a palace poverty, but they can only respond to their emotions, and their feelings shine through their pictures.

Photo-journalism, which really came into its own in the 1930s with the emergence of three magazines — *Life*, *Paris Match* and *Picture Post* — has told us more about what has been happening in the world in human terms than any words can describe. Vietnam, the most photographed war in history, claimed the lives of a number of photographers; but their work brought home, in graphic detail, the horror and futility of war.

More has been learned about the way people live through the work of the concerned photographer than any other medium. Television and film record events; the still photograph captures emotions, stopped for a split second but everlastingly.

All pictures taken by concerned photographers have one element in common — compassion. None of them can stand aloof from the subject and use his or her camera objectively; they are *involved*, and their work reflects their involvement.

The News Photograph

Although some pictures of crashed trains, burning buildings and earthquake damage had been taken as early as 1850, the pure 'news' photograph did not come into its own until the turn of the century, after the development of half-tone printing and, more importantly, the invention of wire trans-

mission of pictures in 1907. When telegraphing photographs hundreds of miles within minutes became possible, 'photo-journalism' was born. For the concerned photographer it opened up totally new possibilities.

The impact of a top-rate news photograph was first seen with the picture of Mayor William Gaynor of New York at the moment of being shot by an assassin in 1910. The Mayor was about to board a ship to go on holiday in Europe as an American newspaper photographer arrived. He asked the Mayor to pose for a picture and as he raised his camera two shots were fired from the crowd. In the midst of the confusion the photographer remained calm and his picture of the blood-spattered Mayor lurching into the arms of an aide has become part of photographic history.

However, it is not pure chance that makes historic news photographs; much is demanded of the photographer. Of course he has to be there to witness the event, but news is often made in seconds and the photographer has to be able to react just as quickly.

Twenty-two photographers were waiting on 6th May 1937, when the German dirigible 'Hindenberg' arrived in New Jersey after its first Atlantic crossing. As the giant airship prepared to dock, flames shot from the hull and in less than 60 seconds it had fallen from the air and was strewn over the ground in an unrecognizable heap of burning wreckage. Every one of the photographers got at least one picture of the disastrous moment when the airship exploded.

War photographers

The first known war photographer was an Englishman, Roger Fenton. In a horse-drawn van equipped as a darkroom he went to the Crimean War in 1855 and brought back 360 photographs, a formidable achievement in the light of the diffi-

A mobile darkroom as used by Roger Fenton during the Crimean War. Negatives were developed within ten minutes of exposure.

culties under which he was obliged to work and the fact that his van often drew the fire of the Russian artillery.

In those days, of course, the 'action picture' was technically impossible, but Fenton had an unerring talent for reportage and his pictures of the trenches, the havoc of war and spirit of the soldiers showed the Victorians, for the first time, what life was like at the front.

Roger Fenton was not the kind of man to be deterred by problems. To get facilities to travel from one location to another, he took portraits of senior officers posing in gallant attitudes. In his van he carried 36 cases of equipment, including more than 600 photographic plates. Before he could start work, he had to coat his plates with collodion solution and clamp them, still damp, into light-proof holders. When he had taken his pictures he rushed back to his van to develop, dry and varnish them before the image faded, while outside the battle continued around him. On one occasion a cannon-ball whistled straight through the side of the van while he was working and the light that came in through the hole ruined a complete set of plates.

Fenton, a former landscape and portrait photographer, tended to avoid subjects which portrayed too graphically for Victorian taste, the grim reality of war in terms of death and destruction. That task was left, nearly ten years later, to Mathew Brady, an American who recruited teams of photographers to cover the American Civil War. These men turned their cameras on devastated battlefields, the dead and the wounded, the senseless slaughter and destruction; their pictures were the first true precursors of modern-day war photography.

During the First World War, official photographers were attached to the armed forces on both sides for the first time but, curiously, their pictures were not widely published at the time and therefore made little impression on the public.

Perhaps the war was too horrific for the public appetite, perhaps the scenes of soldiers in the stinking trenches face to face across No Man's Land changed too little during those four long years. Whatever the reason, few pictures emerged from the holocaust other than those showing bomb-blasted landscapes, or soldiers standing in endless seas of mud.

It was very different in the Second World War, during which some of the greatest photographs were taken. Men like Robert Capa, Eliot Elisofon, Edward Steichen, David Douglas Duncan and W. Eugene Smith set new standards not only in their chosen craft but in personal courage and dedication. They also showed that there were more ways of photographing a war than directing their cameras at bombs, guns, smoke and flame; the agony of war can be portrayed just as effectively in the face of one unknown soldier.

These were not the only men producing historic photographs during those years. Some of the best pictures were taken by unnamed soldiers and sailors assigned to photographic duties. Amongst the best were Stuka dive-bombers flying over Poland taken from the cockpit of a plane in the formation, a study of a US Navy pilot standing on the wing of his plane, exhausted German storm-troopers taking a break while a Russian village burns behind them, the attack on Pearl Harbour.

One of the most heart-rending pictures of the war was taken by the famous Russian photographer Dmitri Baltermants in the Crimea where, nearly a century before, the profession of war photography was born. Called simply *Sorrow, 1942*, it shows grief-stricken Russian women searching for relatives among the bodies lying on a muddy battlefield.

Compassion Through the Lens

War is not the only subject that occupies the concerned photographer. From the beginning the plight of the poor, the under-privileged and the sick has been documented by the camera. During the 1870s a Scotsman named John Thompson took an unforgettable series of pictures of street life in London — junk shops, boot blacks, ice cream sellers and so on — which not only showed the poverty but also the dignity and vitality of cockney people.

One of the first photographers to use his talent as a means of effecting social change was an American, Lewis Hine. A geography teacher at a private school in New York, Hine did not take up photography until he was nearly 30 years old. But after taking a set of pictures to illustrate the living conditions of poor European immigrants, he gave up his teaching job to devote all his time to photographing social injustice in America. His most famous pictures, taken after the turn of the century, exposed the appalling plight of children working in cotton mills and underground in mines. They played a considerable part in the passing of the Child Labor Law.

Hine was different from most of the previous photographers who had attempted social reportage — they were mainly interested in simply documenting life as it was at that time; Hine wanted to change it. He influenced a new generation of determined and forceful young photographers, suddenly aware of their power.

This power was to manifest itself most strikingly

nearly forty years later when American negroes began their long struggle for equality. At every step of the way their cause was photographed and the pictures were flashed to media throughout the world. The first picture of impact was, perhaps, one taken in 1937 of a negro chained to a tree in Mississippi after being tortured and lynched. Of recent pictures perhaps the most striking is that of the balcony in Memphis where Dr Martin Luther King lay dying while outstretched arms pointed to his fleeing assassin. The millions of photographs taken in between these two form a historical documentary record.

Bill Brandt's collection of pictures entitled *The English At Home*, taken during the early 1930s, was designed to illustrate the enormous gap between rich and poor. Mostly taken in the coal-mining towns in the North of England, the photographs illustrate the hardship and squalor of the Depression years; looking at them today they poignantly convey the cold, the dirt, the hunger and the misery.

In America at the same time, two women were compiling their own documentation of similar conditions. In 1932, Dorothea Lange, a portrait photographer from San Francisco, turned to subjects of social concern after seeing a bread line in the street opposite her studio. Her pictures of the appalling conditions in the depressed areas of America did much to awaken the nation's conscience; she had no special techniques, only a deep compassion for the plight of the poor and the underprivileged. Margaret Bourke-White spent most of her time in the Southern states putting together an astonishing portfolio of pictures illustrating the life of American negroes — most tellingly, those working on chain gangs. In 1937 she published the pictures in a book simply entitled *You Have Seen Their Faces*.

On rare occasions, a single photograph covers many different, conflicting emotions. Henri Cartier-Bresson called it the 'decisive moment' and demonstrated it perfectly in his historic picture of a Gestapo informer being identified in a displaced persons' camp in Germany in 1945. The informer stands at a desk, head bowed, while the woman who has identified her spreads her arms in a sweeping gesture of contempt. The official sitting at the desk appears stunned, but the faces of the crowd around them register a range of extraordinarily different emotions.

Eugene Smith's concern and involvement with his subject was so important to him that he hoped, idealistically, that every picture he took would be a contribution to the mutual understanding of peoples, one for another. In 1951 he produced a

Candid street scene early this century.

classic of a new form of photographic expression which *Life* magazine described as an 'essay' — it was a marvellous picture story of life in a poor Spanish village. Smith spent a year living in the community to be accepted as one of them in order to understand their lives and customs.

Such dedication to a subject is not unusual, even today with fewer magazines on the market and less money available to sponsor such ambitious projects. There will always be work for the concerned photographer, for there is no better instrument for documenting the human condition than a camera and compassion.

Roger Fenton is known principally for his photographic records of the Crimean War. But as official government photographer he was obliged to return with rather glamorous and romantic photographs for the sake of national face, so his pictures in fact show nothing of the true horror of war. At home, however, he worked on portraits, still lifes, landscapes and social themes; and like John Thomson, Scottish-born photographer, found a certain definite dignity in both human effort and poverty, as in his portrait of a knife-grinder *below*. *Far right* Two examples of Thomson's work dating from the 1850s and depicting the poor of London's streets: rag sellers and a group which includes white-bearded shoeshineman Jacobus Parker, famous local character of the time. Many such pictures were probably carefully posed in spite of their natural appearance.

Overleaf **A powerful portrait of three uniformed soldiers from Eugene Smith's poignant series *The Spanish Village,* investigating the themes of life and death in a small community. *Below* the blank and terrified faces of starved, tortured prisoners behind the barbed wire of Buchenwald, as seen by liberating troops and concerned photographer Margaret Bourke-White in 1945.**

On page 65, undoubtedly Robert Capa's most famous single picture, taken from his reportage of the Spanish Civil War, 1936: the now classical shot of man and war — a Spanish soldier at the very moment of death, killed by a machine-gun bullet through the head. Below this, Dessau 1945; and in a displaced person's camp, an enraged refugee exposes an informer for the Gestapo: Photo, Henri Cartier-Bresson.

Robert Capa took some of the most moving front-line pictures of war in Israel prior to creation of the State in 1948, and also recorded in a compassionate series the influx of Jewish refugees from all over the world. Here, a moment of anguish for a Jewish Yemenite child experiencing the strangeness and upheaval of arrival at an immigration camp.

Above right **Mourners by a grave in Nam Dinh, Indo-China 1954, when Capa was killed on his final, dangerous mission.** *Right* **Civil war, and photographer Don McCullin, also famed for his candid shots of war in Vietnam and Cyprus, witnesses the terrified reaction of residents as soldiers charge after a violent incident in Londonderry, Northern Ireland.**

Concern at the plight of certain women workers at the beginning of the century — engaged as they sometimes were in heavy, dirty and poorly paid work — is depicted in two photographic portraits *below* by H. Nicholls which also convey the dignity of effort. *Right* The candid portraiture of Henri Cartier-Bresson who had an amazing gift for capturing the most fleeting expressions and gestures of his subject's personality and outlook. *Top* Prostitutes, Mexico 1934: *bottom* Sunday on the Banks of the Marne. Photo-reportage had become an art form.

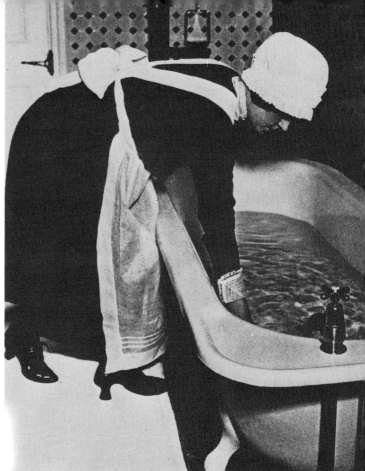

Examples of Bill Brandt's extensive photographic documentation of English social life in the 1930s. *Above* **Parlourmaid and undermaid ready to serve dinner, and preparing a bath.**

Below **Customers at the Crooked Billet public house, Tower Hill, London; and an unemployed miner's child.** *Right* **The Depression — a coal searcher wends his way home.**

With outstanding and characteristic qualities
of technical simplicity, deliberate lack of
stylization and above all enormous compassion,
many of Lord Snowdon's photographic essays
have investigated serious sociological problems
—spina bifida, old age and mental illness
among them. *Above* An old man, barefooted by
the sea, from a series entitled *Loneliness,* 1966.
Right Hope, dignity and warmth in aging
features.

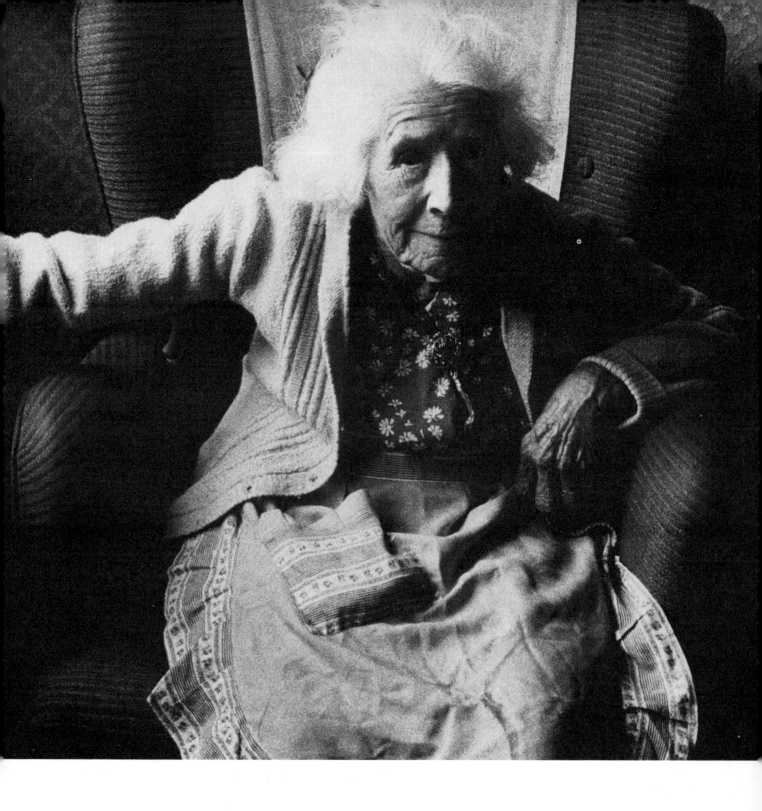

The Nude

No single subject has been photographed more than the female nude. She appears on thousands of calendars throughout the world, in advertisements, newspapers, books and magazines. There are probably more nude photographic models working today than ever before and the demand for them is increasing all the time. Yet, paradoxically, the nude is thought to be the most difficult subject to photograph successfully.

Michael Boys, one of Britain's foremost nude photographers, explains the problem like this: 'A successful picture of a nude has to mix the atmosphere of sexuality with time, place and light and the graphics of body drawing. It is not so much concerned with eroticism; her nudity, or the perfection of her body, is not significant.

'What is important is that she has got the capacity in her mind to excite, to convey perhaps something of what she is thinking, something of what is happening, or has just happened or is going to happen, something of life as it is at that time. If she can't do that, you might just as well be photographing a string of sausages.'

Most photographers agree that eroticism is not a particularly powerful element in nude photography; in fact many of them consistently draw their inspiration not from the entire body, but a small part of it — a single crease in the flesh or the juxtaposition of limb and torso.

Harry Callahan's delightful picture of 'Eleanor', taken in 1947, shows a narrow section of a girl's back from the base of the spine to just above her knees. All the photograph shows is four more or less straight lines against the white of the skin. It is a design picture as much as a nude, but it is also full of humour and charm.

Distortion

Modern wide-angle and long-focus lenses have enabled photographers to use the nude almost as a piece of sculpture. In Bill Brandt's classic series of a nude girl lying near the surf on a pebble beach, one never sees the complete woman — she appears as a smooth white shape in stark contrast to the texture of the beach and in some of the pictures she appears as much rock as woman. André Kertész, one of the most celebrated nude photographers ever, was also fascinated by distortion. He used reflections in curved mirrors and water to change the shape of his models, or an extremely wide-angled lens which grossly distorted the perspectives of the body.

Early photographers of the nude had neither the inclination nor the facilities for such experiments. All their attention was occupied by posing the model and getting her to keep still for up to ten minutes while the film was exposed.

The first nude photographs were taken by an enterprising Frenchman named Noël Lerebours in 1840, only a year after Daguerre had perfected his historic process. Most of his studies were used by painters for reference, but it was not long before models were being posed in the style of Renaissance paintings for so-called 'art photographs'.

Victorian Prudery

Nude photographs were soon widely accepted in France and the United States, but in Britain Victorian prudery made life much more difficult for the aspiring nude photographer. Although in some circles it was fashionable for women to compile an album of nude studies of their female friends (taken by a lady photographer, of course), most people were convinced that no decent woman would take her clothes off in front of a camera. Those who did were usually considered to be prostitutes or pathetic wretches forced against their will to pose. It was not until the turn of the century that photographers were really able to abandon the pseudo-artistic approach to the nude which made her look more like a statue than a living woman.

New ground was broken in 1906 by Alvin Coburn with a picture that imitated Rodin's sculpture, 'The Thinker'. The model, amazingly, was George Bernard Shaw, although it was not that which made the picture different but the clever use of soft focus and diffuse lighting. Edward Steichen, one of the founding fathers of modern photography, also showed the way for future generations of photo-

graphers with a series of striking nude studies as much concerned with art as was the work of Michelangelo.

Search for Truth

It was Edward Weston who made nude photography acceptable to all levels of society. Using the simplest of equipment — a large view camera, tripod and exposure meter — and natural sunlight, his pictures of the nude reflect the incomparable clarity of his vision of natural forms.

After Weston, the search for truth distinguished the best nude photographers. Bill Brandt even went to the extent of using an old Kodak pinhole camera because he felt that techniques had progressed so quickly that no one had sufficiently explored the possibilities of earlier developments. The sculptural, surrealistic pictures that resulted are still regarded as landmarks in the history of nude photography.

Perhaps the man most recently responsible for popularizing the nude in photography is Sam Haskins. *Cowboy Kate*, his first brilliant book of evocative, whimsical nude studies built around loosely-knit stories, became a best-seller all over the world and inspired thousands of other photographers, both professional and amateur, to follow his example.

An appealing blend of romanticism and realism, most early nude photographs were posed to resemble contemporary paintings.

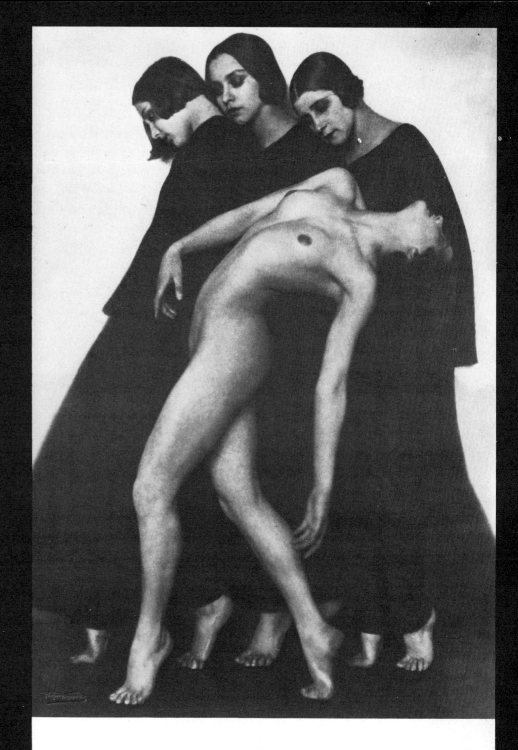

Far left **Two early nude photographs — one semi-clothed and posed on a tigerskin rug, the other an allegory of childhood innocence — both taken during the 1850s. Nude models were in fact among the camera's first subjects: and artists like Delacroix and Courbet soon realized that the resulting prints could be very helpful reference for life studies in paintings.** *Left* **A nude photographic study by Watson, 1856; and** *above* **in somewhat startling contrast, a later lithe dancing form posed against the starkness of three dark, cloaked figures, by Demarchy.**

77

Below A beautifully toned print in which body curves flow in serene composition. Robert Demarchy was one of the Photo-Secessionists, an American school whose work was regularly published in the magazine *Camera* first founded in 1902 by Stieglitz. The school varied widely in style, but always remarkable was a certain poetic quality to the photographs. *Right* Nude by Stieglitz and Clarence White: and *overleaf* their famous, almost mystical study, *Torso*. In complete contrast, we see in the nude photography of Edward Weston (as in the study reproduced on page 81, taken 1936) the characteristic refined lines of so much of his work. Only occasionally did Weston use artificial light, far preferring the qualities of natural sunlight; and the equipment he favoured for capturing the essence of natural form was always the most basic and technically simple.

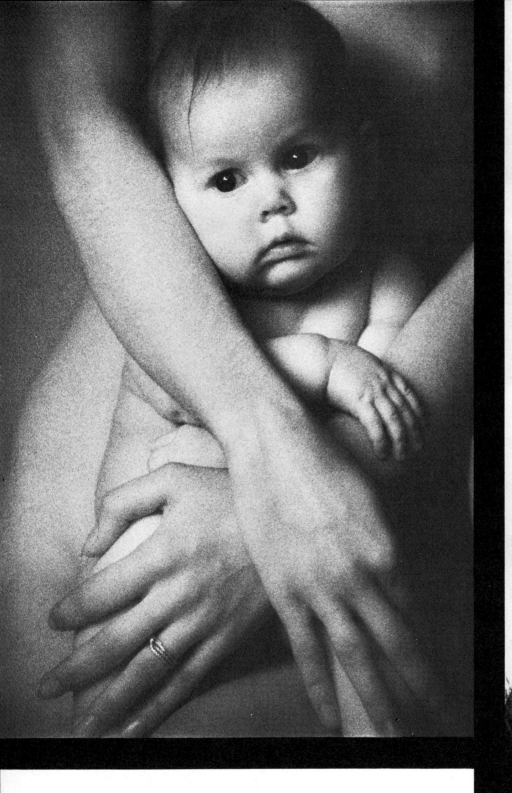

In a Portrait of Infancy, Patrick Lichfield manages to capture the very tenderness of maternal protection. Mother's hands are crossed as though to envelop baby's innocence, and skin tones blend almost as if one. Meanwhile *right* **the exhilaration and joy at being alive and an uninhibited pride in the human form are conveyed in John Garrett's highly satisfying portrait of two generations.**

Above **Michael Boys,** one of Britain's principal nude photographers, believes that far more important than perfection of body form or blatant eroticism is that the model should convey an atmosphere of sexuality and put over her feelings and mood at the time, which the photographer can then emphasize with skilful use of light. *Left* Dramatic lighting gives an added illusion of movement to a nude by Mike Berkofsky.

Bill Brandt, also famous for candid pictorial documentation of English social life in the 30s, first began to experiment with the nude when he discovered an old, almost primitive mahogany Kodak with wide-angle lens and miniscule aperture in a Covent Garden junk shop. It was an all-important find. Disenchanted with results achieved using modern cameras, he was soon creating nude compositions like the two shown here: surrealistic shots and also several abstract, distorted forms set against cliff and seashore, looking much like sculptures.

The Creative Camera

There was certainly little love lost between early photographers and artists. Many painters despised photography as a purely mechanical gimmick which required no artistic skill of any kind. Photographers tended to reply by scoffing at the painstaking efforts of painters to reproduce reality; with a camera they could capture a perfect image within minutes, so what, they asked, was the point of labouring for hours with crayon or paint?

The controversy revolved around one central question: was photography art? Photographers, not unnaturally, immediately proclaimed themselves as new artists, but ruined their case by slavishly copying the technique of the painters.

Art photography, in its early form, normally involved setting up in a studio a picture that closely resembled a classic painting. Allegorical and mythological scenes were popular — models draped in swathes of chiffon posed against cardboard cut-out parapets in front of crudely-painted backdrops. In the main, they were a disaster artistically, although they often found favour with the public.

In 1857 Oscar Rejlander, a Swedish painter turned photographer, produced the biggest and most ambitious allegorical photograph ever taken. Composed from more than 30 negatives, it was called *The Two Ways Of Life* and showed a number of figures in classic poses with 'Industry' represented on one side, 'Dissipation' on the other and 'Penitence' in the middle. Although many people were shocked at the semi-nudity of some of the models, Queen Victoria thoroughly approved of its moral tone and bought it as a present for Prince Albert.

Pictorial Photography

Another eminent photographer of the day, Henry Peach Robinson, was producing composite pictures in a style which became known as 'pictorial photography'. Robinson's technique was almost to negate the camera. He sketched the design for his picture and then photographed it in stages, sticking each part into place and then re-photographing the whole when it was complete. His bucolic and

sentimental scenes proved very popular, particularly in Britain, and led to a rash of similar photographs with titles like *The Baron's Feast*, *A Scene In The Tower* and *Pray God, Bring Father Safely Home*.

Partly as a result of the 'pictorialists', the uneasy relationship between art and photography began slowly to improve. It had become clear that the camera would not be able to compete with art on equal terms and that the fine, majestic works of the great painters could not be satisfactorily imitated by photography.

At the same time, increasing numbers of painters began to realize that photography was a useful tool — it gave them the opportunity of making a number of life studies quickly and cheaply to use as reference and avoid long and expensive sessions with models.

A few decades had yet to pass before the realization dawned that photography and art were allies rather than enemies. The photographers had to discard the shackles of thinking of photographs in terms of paintings. They were then free to explore the potential of the camera and create, for the first time, photographs that would stand on their own merits as works of art. Similarly, painters discovered that photography effectively relieved them of the burden of realistic representation and that they, too, were free to experiment.

New Realism

This happened in the last twenty years of the nineteenth century when a number of photographers rebelled against the artificiality of the 'pictorialists' and set off in pursuit of realism. The leader was a dogmatic Englishman, Peter Henry Emerson. His philosophy was that photographs should not sentimentalize, but be faithful to,

There are obvious similarities in the work of Pre-Raphaelite painters and the photography of Oscar Rejlander with his liking for allegory and moralistic pictures. As with his work for *The Wayfarer* he used sketches and negatives in a combination print.

Nature with nothing added and nothing changed from reality. To this end, he spent nearly ten years photographing the life and landscape of the Norfolk Broads and his pictures made a significant contribution towards changing the direction of photography.

Despite Emerson's vociferous proclamations that there should be no link between the photograph and the painting, photographers were nevertheless being influenced by painters, notably by the French Impressionists. In 1890 George Davison exhibited a beautiful Impressionist photograph of an onion field with cottages clustered in the background. By using soft-focus and a rough surface paper, he blurred the image and revived the long-standing argument about whether a soft photograph was better than a sharp one.

Around the turn of the century new printing processes advanced the photographer's claim to art. By controlling the pigment of the picture during the development stage and by altering the print manually with a brush, pencil or rubber, photographers discovered that they were able to produce totally new effects — photographs that did not look like photographs. Thus, photography and art were finally joined and a distinction was made between the amateur with a box camera taking 'snaps' and the serious photographer dedicated to expanding the horizons of photographic art.

A Frenchman, Robert Demachy, led the way. With barely concealed contempt for the 'snap', Demachy experimented endlessly not only with his camera but in the darkroom to produce a variety of effects to enhance the final print. His photograph of an open car speeding along a dusty road in 1904 showed clearly what could be done: by using a rough-textured paper and coating it with gum bichromate which could be thickened or thinned with hot water during the printing process, he blotted out much of the detail and achieved an image that captured speed more effectively than ever before.

Ending The Doubts

It was an American, Alfred Stieglitz, who finally dispelled any lingering doubts that photography was able to stand on its own as a creative art. Stieglitz devoted his life to photography and did more than any other individual to foster widespread acceptance of photography as an art form; he took many brilliant pictures himself, opened an art gallery in New York to promote the work of avant-garde photographers, edited the enormously influential magazine *Camera Work* between 1903

The art-photography of Henry Peach Robinson.

and 1917 and became a towering figure in the history of photography. Some of his best pictures were of Nature; he called them 'equivalents' because he saw them as external statements of his inner feelings.

After Stieglitz, the doors were open for a new wave of photographers, ready to break with traditional subjects and to introduce a totally new concept to modern photography. Paul Strand produced wonderful still lifes of ordinary domestic subjects — a pile of kitchen bowls or a white picket fence. Man Ray made startling pictures, which he called 'Rayographs', by simply laying out simple objects on photographic paper and then turning on a light. Laszlo Moholy-Nagy experimented with double printing, multiple exposures and striking photomontage.

Their work was followed, in the 1920s, by yet another 'movement', this time called 'New Objectivity'. It was pioneered by a German, Albert Renger-Patzsch, who called upon photographers to leave 'art to the artists . . . let us try by means of photography to create photographs which can stand alone . . . without borrowing from art.' Renger-Patzsch was fascinated by the beauty of everyday objects and his close-ups isolated the subject from its surroundings and showed it with complete clarity and startling realism.

Instrument of Love

Soon photographers were discussing their work in almost mystical terms that would have been ridiculed not many years before. Ansel Adams, famous for his majestic landscape pictures, described a photograph as 'an instrument of love and revelation . . . it must see beneath the surface and record the qualities of nature and humanity which live . . . in all things.' One of his disciples, Minor White, took the philosophy a step further — his extraordinary close-ups of pieces of driftwood, rock formations or icicles were, he said, 'inner landscapes' revealed by 'self-discovery through a camera'. Aaron Siskind further startled the photographic world with almost three-dimensional pictures of texture — he turned peeling posters, stone walls or crumbling plaster into abstract works of art.

Throughout its history, photography has constantly been changing direction, sometimes moving into totally new areas, sometimes turning full circle to take up again the challenges met by earlier photographers. Only one thing is certain — whichever direction it is moving now or moves in the future, one fact has been established beyond dispute: photography *is* art.

Soft focus and a blurred image give an impressionistic effect to Davison's Onion Field, 1890.

Above **Harlech Castle by George Davison. A muted photograph, he argued, was far more pleasing than a sharp one. Acceptance of photography as art was now a matter of considerable controversy. Emerson believed** that photographs should not romanticize but be faithful to Nature. *Below* **A Rushy Shore by Henry Emerson, dated 1887:** *right* **one of his many realistic and social pictures depicting life on an East Anglian farm.**

Demarchy was another to rebel against naturalistic photography. He stated emphatically that a photograph could only be deemed a work of art if it resembled a painting in style and composition. *Au bord du lac* and *Speed* *below* are examples of his work. He would eliminate detail using rough paper with a coating of gum arabic to produce an effect which the camera on its own could not possibly have achieved. *Right* Street scenes by Stieglitz. His creative success did not involve retouching, but is generally put down to patient waiting for what Stieglitz himself called the 'moment of equilibrium.'

Above A composition in reds taken in
Botswana by photographer John Goldblatt.
Particularly remarkable here is a
complete absence of supplementary colour
and the juxtaposition of similarly toned
subjects, animal and man-made. With
recording of such pleasing visual coincidence
and detail, photography becomes art. *Right*
Toby Molenaar's starkly graphic picture of
an old woman at the window with emphasis on
texture and shape is somehow reminiscent
of Edward Weston's close-up of a Californian
church door, reproduced overleaf.

Edward Weston, originally a romantic photographer, later changed his style under the influence of painter Diego Rivera. During the 1920s he began exhibiting the textured still life and landscape photography using natural lighting for which he now is famed. *Below* Light falls across a church door in Hornitos, California, 1904. *Bottom* **A Sweet Pepper, 1930.** *Right* **The magnificent waves and patterns of sand dunes.**

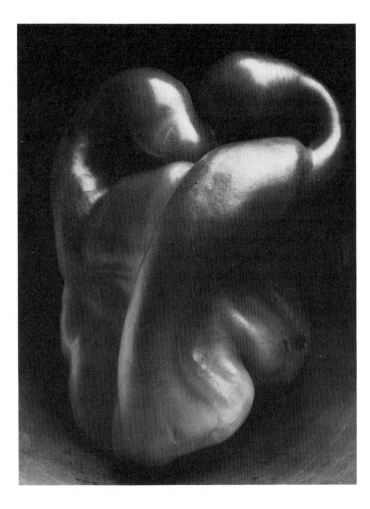

Above **An unusual still life by Roger Phillips in which he deliberately set out to simulate an artistic effect with subtle use of double exposure to allow the very texture of wood and cloth to penetrate the central objects.** *Right* **Harry Bakkers chose to shoot these delightfully nostalgic, peeling papier-maché dolls through the panes of an Antwerp antique shop window, giving an added impression of both age and of mystery.**

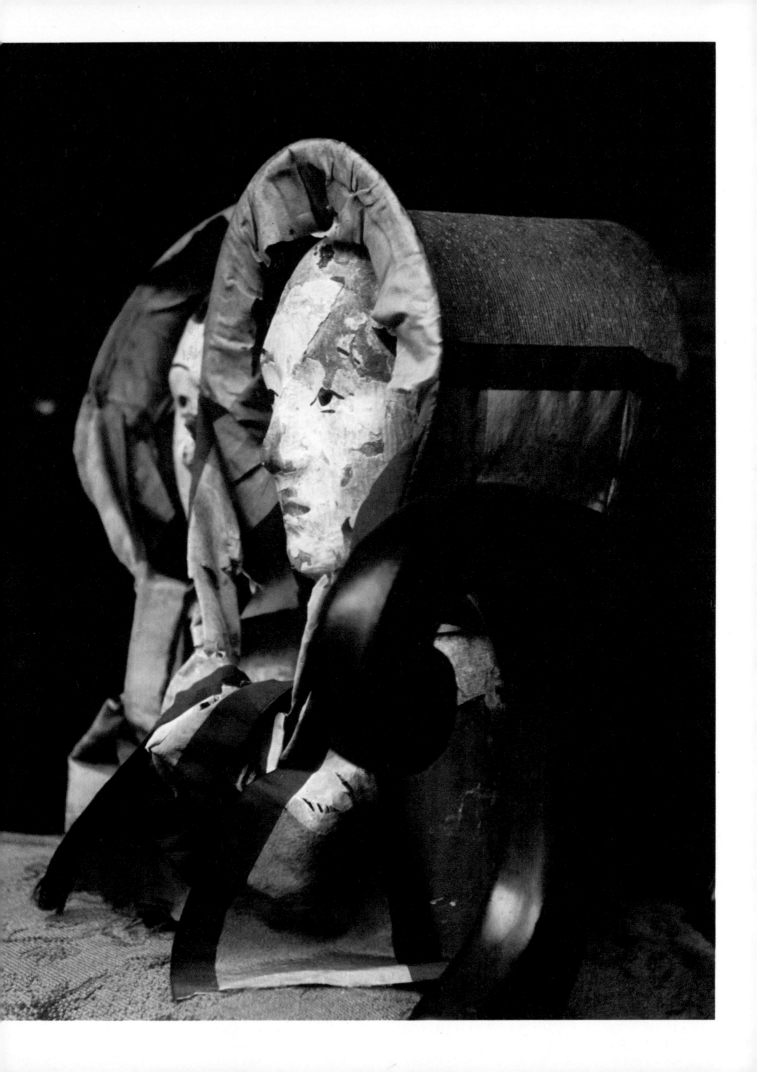

Left **Joseph Van Wormer sees an abstract black and white design in Nature and photographs a flock of snow geese.** *Above* **Also abstract but rather more contrived is this vortograph by Alvin Langdon Coburn, produced using mirrors reflecting multiple images with such effect of distortion that the original object photographed cannot be recognized. 'Why should not the camera also throw off the shackles of conventional representation and attempt something fresh and untried?' wrote Coburn in 1916.**

Not rickety, tumble-down shacks, just an illusion: for what Adam Woolfitt has in fact photographed *above* is the distorted reflection of quaint Amsterdam houses by the waterside. *Overleaf* The impressionistic rippling effect of a mystical composition *Sierra Madre,* surprisingly by Margaret Bourke-White, most widely remembered for her outstandingly concerned reportages.

Two recent compositions by Eric Howard
which involve both painting and photography.
Left A painted rainbow background is enhanced
by golden light and then put out of focus so
that colours blend. On the final print, the
hairline is given additional definition with
careful use of brushwork. *Above* Sun and moon
were suspended against the background and the
Gemini face painted in by a skilful make-up
artist before both art and photography created
the final illusion of heavenly twins.

Above **Fantastic surrealistic composition
including a self-portrait by British theatrical
photographer Angus McBean, taken in 1949.**
Right **An intriguing photo-montage taken for
the British magazine *Queen* by leading
American still-life photographer Lester
Bookbinder. Now turn the page for an exciting
piece of colourful abstract art — which is in
fact a photograph of bubbles of liquid detergent
in a milk bottle! Tony Copeland has used
flat, soft lighting to emphasize these colours
and their reflections in the bubbles.**

Contrast in texture, strange perspective and dream-like distortion all combine in the compositions by Bill Brandt. Fingers are dramatic cliffs beside small pebbles, and legs are dunes of sand. It is hard to classify this work either as straightforward nude photography or as scenic shots. Brandt chose to aim for intimacy of his nudes with the environment and closely related body shape to natural elements like pebbles and rocks.

Photo-reportage is considered an art form by many people. *Above* **Steve Herr makes social comment in photographing a piece of pavement art found in a subway at London's Hyde Park Corner. But what, one wonders, would early realist schools have made of Malcolm Robertson's recent and highly impressionistic photograph of an artist at his easel** *left* **taken through the glass of a car window on a drizzly day in order to soften any possible final sharpness in the printed image? Surely a neat visual comment on the question of whether photography can indeed be classified as art.**

Great Names

Every list of great photographers has one weakness — those names which have been left out. In the field of photography so much has been achieved by so many that no book could mention them all. The men and women mentioned on these pages have all made great contributions to the art, technique or development of photography. Other great contributors to specific fields of photography are mentioned more appropriately in other chapters. But, inevitably, many are not mentioned at all.

NADAR, or Gaspard Felix Tournachon, was one of the first professional photographers. Born in Paris in 1820, he was a great showman and a keen balloonist. Most of his early pictures were portraits of famous people; his studio, with his name painted in red in huge letters on the wall outside, was a meeting place for Paris intelligentsia. He was a pioneer in many fields — he was the first to experiment with electric light for portraiture, the first to take aerial photographs from a balloon and the first to take underground pictures in the catacombs of Paris. In 1863, he had built the biggest balloon in Europe and announced plans for an aerial survey of the whole of France, but the technical difficulties of photography at that time made the scheme impractical. He died in 1910. His early portraits are thought to be his best work.

NADAR

DAVID OCTAVIUS HILL and ROBERT ADAMSON met in 1843 when Hill, a painter of some repute, decided to start work on a massive group portrait of the first General Assembly of the newly-formed Free Church of Scotland. Adamson had recently opened a Calotype studio in Edinburgh and it was suggested he should take Calotype portraits of the clergymen so that Hill could copy them for the faces in the picture. The deal was agreed, but the Calotypes turned out so well that Hill turned to photography with Adamson. They were curious partners — Hill a bluff extrovert in his forties and Adamson a thin, frail youth in his early twenties. But in the space of five years they produced more than 2,000 pictures of great quality. The majority are forceful portraits, but the two men also captured the charm of life in small seaside villages near their home. When Adamson died at the age of 27 Hill returned to painting.

JULIA MARGARET CAMERON

JULIA MARGARET CAMERON (1815—1879) remains one of the most extraordinary figures in the history of photography. A dynamic, intelligent woman with boundless energy, she brought up her own six children and several orphans before turning to photography as a hobby at the age of 48. She converted a coal shed into a darkroom, and made a chicken coop into a studio and began to produce some of the finest Victorian portraits. She photographed everyone, from servants to celebrities such as Lord Tennyson and Darwin. Many of her pictures have a pre-Raphaelite quality about them and she was one of the first photographers to exploit the potential of the close-up. Her technical knowledge was thin and many of her pictures were out of focus — but they have a quality of grace and warmth which endures today.

PAUL MARTIN (1864—1942) was the first 'candid cameraman'. He described his aim in photography as a search for 'the real snapshot — that is, people and things as the man in the street sees them'. He was gadget mad, and modified his camera to make it as unobtrusive as possible, even to the extent of hiding it in a briefcase and muffling the noise of the shutter. Thus armed, he toured the streets of London snapping the 'ordinary people' out and about at their work or enjoying themselves at the seaside. His 'London by night' pictures, shot in the winter of 1895—96, were the first of their kind.

PETER HENRY EMERSON (1856—1936) was one of the first photographers to attack publicly the fashion for photographs attempting to emulate paintings. He urged a return to Nature for inspiration, and spent ten years in East Anglia photographing the rustic life and landscape. In 1889 he published a book explaining his view that photographs must be faithful to reality and nothing should be altered or added by the photographer. Two years later, however, he abruptly changed his opinions and declared that naturalistic photography was 'dead'. Despite this, his ideas are still a strong influence on modern photographers.

ALFRED STIEGLITZ (1864—1946), an American, pioneered the concept of photography as art. Editor of the influential magazine *Camera Work* between the years 1903 and 1917, he also owned an art gallery in New York where the work of many photographers was exhibited. He is best known for his pictures of Nature — photographs which he called 'equivalents' because he saw in them the expression of his innermost feelings.

EDWARD WESTON (1886—1958) made his reputation as a photographer with soft-focus, romantic portraits of Hollywood stars. In the 1920s, at the very peak of his success, he abruptly closed his studio in California and went to Mexico for three years, after which he completely changed his style as a photographer. His sharp, objective landscapes and revealing close-ups of unusual natural forms made his work world-famous. In 1937 he became the first photographer to win a Guggenheim Fellowship and with it he took a remarkable series of pictures of the American West.

BILL BRANDT is generally considered to be Britain's greatest photographer. Born in 1905, he started his career in photo-journalism. In 1936 he published an unforgettable documentary record titled *The English at Home* which perfectly illustrated the great gap between the rich and poor. His famous picture of an unemployed miner searching for coal has been published all over the world. When he turned to portraiture, his pictures took on a strong surrealistic quality, probably from the influence of Man Ray, the surrealist painter and photographer, under whom he had studied in Paris in the 1920s. Always original, his brilliant pictures of nudes showed the female form in an entirely new light — the strange, unreal shapes he produced were described as 'a prolonged meditation on the mystery of forms'.

BILL BRANDT

HENRI CARTIER-BRESSON is as much a legend as a photographer. Undoubtedly the most influential photo-journalist ever, he has an extraordinary instinct for capturing the most telling moment in any situation, no matter how ordinary. His classic picture *Sunday on the Banks of the Marne* perfectly conveys the atmosphere of a French working-class family outing. His working methods are as well known as his pictures — he always composes his photographs in the view-finder of his camera and having done so, never allows the prints to be cropped. He describes the success of his pictures as being due to his ability to capture the 'decisive moment'. In any situation, he says 'there is one moment at which the elements in motion are in balance. Photography must seize upon this moment.'

CECIL BEATON

CECIL BEATON is best known for his photographs of celebrities. In the 1930s he created a new style of portraiture in which the sitter formed only a part of the whole picture. His fashion photographs have a romance and elegance which has seldom been bettered. It is a characteristic of a great photographer that he can still produce fine pictures even in totally unfamiliar surroundings. On the outbreak of the Second World War, Beaton exchanged the glamorous world of fashion for the rather different role of official photographer and his pictures of the Blitz in London and the war in the Near and Far East became famous.

YOUSUF KARSH, a refugee from Armenian Turkey, made his reputation by photographing the famous and became so famous himself that it became something of a status symbol to have a portrait taken by 'Karsh of Ottawa'. He was obsessed with the quality of greatness and attempted in his pictures to capture what he called the 'inward power' that showed the source of the sitter's greatness. Part of his technique was complete control over whoever he was photographing — when Winston Churchill refused to remove his cigar for a picture, Karsh plucked it from his lips.

ROBERT CAPA was undoubtedly the world's most famous war photographer. In 1936, at the age of 23, he began his extraordinary career by photographing the Spanish Civil War. His picture of a Loyalist soldier falling at the moment of death is said to be the most dramatic action photograph ever taken. In the Second World War he was present at most of the major actions. Landing with the Allied troops on D-Day, he turned his back on the German defences to photograph the waves of troops coming in over the beach, but most of the 106 frames he shot were destroyed later by a nervous darkroom assistant. Only eight survived and all became classics. At the end of the war he went to Israel to cover the fighting there and then to Vietnam where, in 1954, he was tragically killed. Characteristically in search of a better picture, he stepped on a land mine and died instantly.

ROBERT CAPA

HENRI CARTIER-BRESSON

Lighting gives a psychedelic feel to this portrait of actor David Warner by Cecil Beaton. The art of photography has come a very long way since the early, rather static portraiture of Nadar and the pre-Raphaelite allegories of Julia Cameron and contemporaries. In the age of the Polaroid, the creative potential of the camera now seems infinite. Who knows what the next century, or even the next few years will bring by way of exciting new techniques . . .